What Others Ar

"Norma Joyce has painted a beautiful and very relatable story of how to choose to live a committed life! She paints great word pictures to show the struggle in choosing to do the right thing and the consequences or rewards of that choice."
JANICE MAYO MATHERS, BEND, OREGON AUTHOR, SPEAKER, NATIONAL BOARD DIRECTOR OF STONECROFT MINISTRIES, INC.

"Every young woman seeks approval, validation, and meaning for her life. Tragically many search in the wrong places such as physical beauty and "worldly success." Here is an authentic, delightful testimony of the grace of God in the midst of a difficult beginning followed by a fairytale dream come true which, in turn, was followed by a deep emptiness. Through many struggles, Norma Joyce finally realized fulfillment is found in a living personal relationship with Jesus Christ who alone fills our empty hearts."
GUDNY MUNRO, WIFE OF DR. JOHN MUNRO, SENIOR PASTOR OF CALVARY CHURCH, CHARLOTTE, NORTH CAROLINA

"Norma Joyce's experiences in the glittering world of beauty pageants were something most girls and women can only imagine, yet they didn't bring lasting happiness or fulfillment. Her relationship with God brings out her physical and spiritual beauty as He created it to be. I commend Norma for making her memoirs public and pray that as you read about her life, you too will find the true essence of the human heart."
LORRAINE MYRHOLM, FORMER EXECUTIVE DIRECTOR, STONECROFT MINISTRIES CANADA

"Norma Joyce (Hickey) Dougherty was and continues to be a goodwill ambassador of her native Prince Edward Island. Her memoir, Island Girl: A Triumph of the Spirit, offers an inspiring account of her race with destiny and how an abiding faith led to the discovery of her true purpose in life."
ALEX B. CAMPBELL, PREMIER OF PRINCE EDWARD ISLAND 1966–1978

"Norma Joyce Dougherty has written her story from the heart; gathering up all the heartaches of disappointment and revealing how Jesus Christ covers them in His love and forgiveness, bringing joy and lasting contentment. Reading this book caused me to consider the wisdom found in God's Word: 'Charm is deceitful and beauty is passing, but a woman who fears the Lord she shall be praised' (Proverbs 31:30).

This former beauty queen writes honestly about how the Lord destroys the ugliness of sin through His redemption and makes life worth living."

DONNA LEE TONEY, A COLLEAGUE OF FRANKLIN GRAHAM FOR THIRTY YEARS, HAS BEEN INVOLVED IN THE MINISTRIES OF SAMARITAN'S PURSE AND THE BILLY GRAHAM EVANGELISTIC ASSOCIATION AND IN LITERARY COLLABORATION SINCE 1982, MOST RECENTLY WITH FRANKLIN GRAHAM ON *A STORY OF SIMPLE GIFTS: OPERATION CHRISTMAS CHILD* AND *SALVATION: THE REASON FOR MY HOPE* WITH BILLY GRAHAM

ISLAND GIRL

A young girl's real-life fairy tale and her personal
and spiritual odyssey to reach the true shoreline

ISLAND GIRL

A Triumph of the Spirit

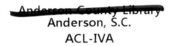
Norma Joyce Dougherty

ELM HILL

A Division of
HarperCollins Christian Publishing

www.elmhillbooks.com

Island Girl
A Triumph of the Spirit

Published in Nashville, Tennessee, by Elm Hill, an imprint of Thomas Nelson. Elm Hill and Thomas Nelson are registered trademarks of HarperCollins Christian Publishing, Inc.

To help with recapping my memories, I am grateful to Google and Wikipedia.com.

Photographs of Miss Dominion of Canada: Used by permission of The Journal Pioneer, Summerside, Prince Edward Island, Canada

Cover photo by Deborah J. Young

Elm Hill titles may be purchased in bulk for educational, business, fund-raising, or sales promotional use. For information, please e-mail SpecialMarkets@ThomasNelson.com.

Scripture quotations marked (niv) are taken from the Holy Bible, New International Version®, NIV®. Copyright © 1973, 1978, 1984 by Biblica, Inc.™ Used by permission of Zondervan. All rights reserved worldwide. www.zondervan.com

Scripture quotations marked (nlt) are taken from the Holy Bible, New Living Translation, copyright © 1996. Used by permission of Tyndale House Publishers, Inc., Wheaton, Illinois 60189. All rights reserved.

"In the Garden" refrain: Used by permission of Public Domain.

Library of Congress Cataloging-in-Publication Data

Library of Congress Control Number: 2018930963

ISBN 978-1-595540935 (Paperback)
ISBN 978-1-595541031 (eBook)

Dedicated to Father and Mother. Your teachings and struggles led me to see and understand that life is not perfect even though we try to make it so, that life is full of successes and failures. We must not be ashamed of our failures but rather learn from them in order to celebrate our successes.

To my husband Bill who is now living in heaven. You were always my greatest cheerleader, never doubting, always encouraging and constantly finding the best in me. I would not be the person I am today if you had not come into my life. Thank you for walking this journey with me over the years and helping me find the triumph within my spirit. I love you with an everlasting love.

To my daughter, Miki. You have been my inspiration since the moment I first held you in my arms. I will never forget how you filled my life with meaning and purpose when I became your mother. I love the way you live life and the way you have become an inspiration to so many other young women through your gifts, your talents, your knowledge, your acceptance, and your love. Keep shining, my love!

To my granddaughter, Lucy, and my grandson, Dylan. I love the way you lead my heart back to fairyland every time we are together. Thanks for always helping me feel like a kid again. You bring a special joy to my heart whenever I see you. There's nothing in this whole wide world like your hugs and kisses.

To all my brothers and sisters. You guys learned long before me the meaning of living life simply one day at a time. My prayer is that you will also find the "kingdom of ideal beauty" and continue to grow in God's love as you tackle your own successes and failures.

A special dedication to my younger sister, Rhea. Your illness and young life raised you to a new level of holiness in my eyes. I miss you so much. A special thanks to my older sister, Barbara Ann, for helping me remember certain details I had long forgotten. You have always been a wonderful guide and a true friend to all of us.

A special thanks to those who have encouraged me in

numerous ways as I worked on this book: to Senator and Mrs. Archibald Johnstone for writing the Foreword. To Scott Sheppard, who spent many hours making my old photos look new again. To Premier Alex B. Campbell, for endorsing my memoir and to other endorsers: Lorraine Potter Kalal, Lorraine Myrholm, Gudny Munro, Mel Graham and Donna Lee Toney. To my dear, dear friends, Ken and Suzanne Friedman, for constantly reading, editing, and stimulating certain details to make the memoir more interesting. My deepest appreciation for your encouragement each and every time I wanted to quit. To a dear friend and author, Janice Mayo Mathers, whose opinions I sought and whose prayers were sustaining. And to Joyce Chadwick, my best friend ever who listens to my heart when I need her most.

CONTENTS

FOREWARD

It is always an occasion when Norma Joyce (Hickey) Dougherty comes to Annandale House to visit with my wife, Phelicia, and me. It was during one of those visits that we discussed the possibility of Norma writing her memoir. Norma states, "It was just that conversation with Archie and Phelicia that finalized my decision. I had actually been thinking about writing my memoir for a long, long time."

I remember well her application for a summer job at Woodleigh Replicas when still a schoolgirl. Regrettably, I had to inform her that at the time all positions were filled. Nor can I forget a telephone call from Mrs. W. H. Smith of Leicester, England, who was my first hostess when I was serving with a

Royal Air Force heavy bomber squadron during World War II. The kind Mrs. Smith was excited, wishing me to know that her television was tuned into a London channel and that she was watching a Prince Edward Island contestant in the Miss World contest. The contestant was Norma Joyce Hickey, already the pride of our island province.

Kensington was the proudest town in the world when in June 1970, Miss Norma Joyce Hickey was crowned Miss Dominion of Canada at the conclusion of the annual pageant held in Niagara Falls, Ontario.

Norma Joyce is the daughter of Mr. and Mrs. Charles Hickey of Darnley, PEI. She attended Kensington Regional High School and, following graduation, took secretarial sciences at Holland College in Charlottetown. During her school days, she was an ardent musician in the Kensington Regional Lions Band and became their drum majorette.

She was first chosen Miss Kensington Lions Club and went on to win the Miss Community Gardens title during the annual harvest festival. Subsequently, her irresistible smile, perfectly proportioned figure, and lively personality won her the title of Miss Dominion of Canada, selected by a distinguished panel of judges as the most beautiful girl in Canada.

I cannot disagree with Mr. Bill Moffatt, a Journal Pioneer newspaper staff writer who, on Wednesday, July 9, 1971 interviewed Norma and described her as a communicative young lady who mixes well with all age groups. "What happens," Mr. Moffatt asked, "when you take a nineteen-year-old girl who has been brought up in a rural community, her new surroundings completely foreign to her, in various countries around the world, with the title of Miss Dominion of Canada and has experienced the 'red carpet' treatment for a whole year?"

This is a question I now feel to be resolved. On interviewing Norma and learning how naturally she reacts to "red carpet" treatment, she gave me some idea of how quickly, even in her first year, she adapted to her new role in a highly exalted environment.

The first impression I got was that Norma is not just a beautiful girl, but rather, she exhibits a personality that is unpretentious, and I think I found out why. With nine brothers and sisters to "bring me down off my high horse" as Norma puts it, it would be hard (if not impossible) for her to put on airs. This is probably one of the reasons she was selected Miss Dominion of Canada. She has a quiet but communicative way about her, and I confirm with Mr. Moffatt this enables her to mix well with all age groups. Norma, however, personally feels that she can communicate better with persons a little older and a little younger than herself, than she can with her own age group.

Presently residing in North Carolina and former wife to the late William "Bill" Dougherty, Norma, who is a member of a prominent Prince Edward Island family, has done a remarkable job in researching her genealogy extending back to Scotland. An interesting fact is that it includes such personalities as Hon. Senator Donald Montgomery and noted author Lucy Maud Montgomery of the Anne of Green Gables series. Lucy Maud was the second cousin to Norma's maternal grandmother, Elizabeth Owen Stewart. Norma is also proud to be the daughter of a mother and father who both served in uniform during World War II and is presently diligently researching their war records.

Norma Joyce (Hickey) Dougherty, former Miss Dominion of Canada and a Miss World contestant, is a lady of undoubted charm, talent, and ability. She has not stopped using her talents all these years. She is a graduate cum laude of the renowned and prestigious Wake Forest University in Winston-Salem, NC with a BA in philosophy and a minor in political science. Not stopping there, Norma has volunteered her many talents for the past twenty years with one of the world's largest women's ministries, Stonecroft Ministries, Inc. Stonecroft.org. She has served in many areas including leadership development, conference planning, mentoring, small-group Bible teaching, initiating new programs including human trafficking awareness and prevention and sitting on the National Board of Directors in Kansas City, Missouri. Norma is also a highly sought-after inspirational speaker for the ministry, introducing many women and young girls to the love of Jesus Christ and the joy of walking in a personal relationship with him as our Lord and Savior. This isn't just a passion for Norma. She sees it as a momentous calling.

Almost forty-eight years have passed since Norma was crowned Miss Dominion of Canada, but Prince Edward Islanders still welcome her summer visits with pride and open arms. I believe we will do the same when she launches her inspirational memoir, Island Girl: A Triumph of the Spirit in the spring of 2018. (Revised and Reprinted)

Many readers young and old will relate to this inspirational rags-to-riches story that begins in poverty, betrayal, and isolation and ends in the discovery of life's most meaningful treasures—deep personal contentment and a truly triumphant spirit. You will be drawn into the honest-to-goodness storytelling approach of this true-to-life personal testimony while it unfolds its many failures, heartfelt victories, and spiritual triumphs. Norma presents the following points of view throughout:

- We are created to seek a meaningful and fulfilling life.

- Life is a journey made up of failures and successes.

- Failures are teaching tools. We are meant to learn from our failures, not to be ashamed of them.

- Successes are heart victories, true treasures that shape an optimistic view of life.

- Failures and successes are meant to work together for our character development, persistence, determination, hope, and contentment.

- God, our creator, is the Source of meaning, significance, value, and fulfillment.

- It is in the Source that we find answers to the questions: Who am I? Where do I belong? What is my purpose in life?

I am more than proud to present this inspirational memoir *Island Girl: A Triumph of the Spirit* to you for your reading pleasure. I believe you, the reader, will find it as I did, an encouraging exploration of the life of one of our own, a young girl who plumbs the depths of her heart and spirit and brings us through to a life of resiliency and triumph to that of a grown woman who truly claims, "I now know who I am, where I belong, and what my purpose is in life. Thanks be to God!"

So let's sound the trumpets for *Island Girl: A Triumph of the Spirit*.

archie Johnstone

— Hon. Archibald Hynd Johnstone,

CD Canadian Senator

(Deceased, November, 2014)

It has always seemed to me, ever since early childhood, amid all the commonplaces of life, I was very near to a kingdom of ideal beauty. Between it and me hung only a thin veil. I could never draw it quite aside, but sometimes a wind fluttered it and I caught a glimpse of the enchanting realms beyond—only a glimpse—but those glimpses have always made life worthwhile.

—L. M. MONTGOMERY, *ANNE OF GREEN GABLES*

INTRODUCTION

You might ask, *Why now?* Why after all these years would I take the time to write my memoir, *Island Girl: A Triumph of the Spirit?* The answer lies within a moment—a moment in time when I stopped wondering, stopped worrying, and started living, living with such a grateful heart that I discovered what I had always been looking for—my true destiny.

When I turned sixty years old, my daughter, Miki, gave me a coffee mug that said, "It took me sixty years to look this good!" We smiled and joked, of course, but the truth is it took me sixty years to feel this good! And when you feel as good as I do, you want to share it with the whole world.

Lucy Maud Montgomery, my maternal grandmother's

second cousin, wrote in Anne of Avonlea, "One can't get over the habit of being a little girl all at once." You could say that was my life's dilemma and my ultimate victory. I lived in fairyland, and while this place is wonderful for a child's imaginary journeys, there comes a time when we must exit fairyland and sojourn into another reality where we become the woman God meant us to become.

My memoir is a real-life fairy tale with an unexpected ending. I did not find happily ever after within fairyland. I found it as I discovered God's heart for his children. I found it when I learned the difference between happiness and joy, the true essence of the human heart, a joy like "none other has ever known."

My story is an inspirational faith-based journey showing how God took a poor farm girl from the smallest province in Canada, Prince Edward Island, and set her on the world's stage. Never leaving me or forsaking me, he held my heart in the palm of his hand, always directing, always leading, always consoling until I recognized that it was he who was "fluttering the thin veil" with his breath, giving me glimpses into the kingdom of ideal beauty. With each glimpse, I found the place my heart calls home.

The kingdom of ideal beauty is our destiny. The path can be a difficult one. I hope, as I share my successes and failures with you, the reader, you will also find the loving face of God within his kingdom of ideal beauty.

> No eye has seen, no ear has heard, no mind has conceived *(the beauty)* what God has prepared for those who love him.
>
> —1 CORINTHIANS 2:9 (NIV)

THE LEGACY

From about ten thousand feet, I looked down on the frozen Northumberland Strait. It was indeed a cold dreary day as I breathed against the frosty window. My gloomy spirit matched my surroundings, and I snuggled ever so deeply under a blanket on the two-engine aircraft that would soon land on Prince Edward Island, my birthplace and the smallest province in Canada. It was December 23, 1986.

The approach to the island did not yield the same breathtaking beauty it does in summer months. Due to a blanket of ice and snow, there was no sparkling blue water from the Atlantic Ocean rushing and breaking against the red rocky cliffs or lapping gently in the quiet coves of this cradle-shaped island. There was no luscious countryside, marked off in fields of varying shades of color, one field different from the other depending on the farmer's choice of crop: yellow, lime, green, or emerald patches bordered with pine trees or dusty country roads. Then, it would look like a patchwork quilt spread out across the ocean, welcoming me back home to rest, recuperate, and enjoy the natural, unspoiled beauty of this cradle by the sea.

A multitude of memories flooded my mind, memories that were colored like the patchy fields with favorable and unfavorable shades, memories that had contributed to my choices in life, memories of events that made me the person I had become at age thirty-five. I thought about my home on the farm, my nine brothers and sisters, my alcoholic father, and my mother who endured all that life had to offer. These thoughts reminded me of the nursery rhyme, "There was an old woman who lived in a shoe. She had so many children she didn't know what to do." Mother is what we called her, and I could remember many times when Mother didn't know what to do. This December day would be one of those times, as the family gathered to lay Father to rest under the patchwork quilt.

*   *   *

Oh, Father, I thought, *why did you disappoint us so much?* I was recalling another time, many years earlier, when my eyes peered through an icy opening in the window of the old farmhouse. I breathed against the opening and rubbed it with my little fingers. I believed if I persisted in keeping the spot from frosting over, if I kept watching through that opening, Father would come home, as he had promised, to take the children to the skating rink. It was a Saturday afternoon, chores were completed; and it was too cold, blustery, and snowy to play outdoors.

But as the day wore on he did not appear and I finally gave up. This was just one of the many promises that had been broken and had left Mother not knowing what to do. But more than that, it left me, at a young age, with a broken heart and an ever-increasing awareness that I could not depend on anyone in life, particularly my father.

He was a strict parent with a loud military style voice gained from having served in the Army during WWII. Often he would come home and roar like Father Bear in the Goldilocks fairy tale when things were not to his liking—a scattering of toys, a meal not prepared, or children not quiet enough. Yes, Father had a way of making his presence known and instilling a fearful respect for authority among his children.

He was certainly a handsome man, tall with a full head of naturally curly hair, an expressive face reflecting a big charming personality, and a hearty laugh that was contagious. Everyone liked Father and thought him to be a very pleasant man. He and Mother met prior to their service in the war—he a soldier in the Army serving overseas and she a secretary in the Air Force. Mother was headquartered at the war department located in Ottawa, Ontario, capital of Canada. They fell in love and dreamed of coming back to Prince Edward Island to raise their family on the rich potato farmlands of this majestic island close to the Atlantic Ocean. And thanks to the military compensation of low-cost land to returning veterans, Father and Mother were able to make their dream come true. (See Appendix A and B for Father's and Mother's War Records.)

Together they purchased one hundred acres of rolling farmland in a small community named Darnley, just up the road from our paternal grandfather's farm. Father and Mother's farm included twenty acres of breathtaking beachfront property on the northern shores of the island. The farm also comprised a large white-shingled house with a green roof, typical of northeastern Canada. A three-story barn capable of housing horses, cattle, pigs and chickens, farm machinery, and lots of bales of hay and straw was situated within close walking distance. A pump house for gathering water was conveniently located between the house and the barn, and an unobtrusively placed outhouse was sheltered in the trees behind the farmhouse, next to an old dilapidated machine shed.

A white picket fence separated the front yard from the apple orchard and a rail fence, intended to keep the farm animals in the barnyard, divided the two areas. However, the chickens managed to have free run all over the place, and this made Mother angry. Murmuring a few unpleasant words she would chase them off the front porch and out of the front yard with her broom. Her displeasure was just loud enough for the children to hear her anger but never loud enough to make out what she was saying.

A red clay driveway, often filled with mud puddles on rainy days, circled in front of the house and into the barnyard. As children we would run and splash through the mud puddles, shouting gleefully at the mess we were making. Needless to say, this too made Mother angry. But this time, her murmuring was loud enough for us to hear, "You children stop running through the mud or I'll make you cut a switch that will sting your little bottoms." Usually this was just a threat, but on occasion cutting our own switches was something Mother made us do when we misbehaved. We thought we were being smart choosing the thinnest one off the bush, but what we didn't realize was the thinner the switch the greater the sting. Therefore when Mother threatened us we listened carefully, but not until we made one last splash just for the fun of it. Yes, it was an idyllic setting for a family homestead set at the end of a long country road with good neighbors, the MacKays, on the other side of the road.

Each year for five consecutive years following their marriage Mother gave birth, always a girl. Father's hope of raising sons and developing his farmland seemed to evade him. The costs of rearing and feeding his family far exceeded the income from the meager production of potatoes he was able to harvest and sell each season. Hired labor and modern machinery were just beyond his reach.

Father kept slipping backward, but he never gave up. He and Mother continued to try for sons and, within two years of the fifth daughter, a son was born, then another. As time went on, there were two more daughters and, last of all, another son. Seven girls and three boys completed Mother's childbearing years, between 1948 and 1963. Born in 1951, I was the fourth daughter in this lineup.

Oh, how I loved my father with the pure love a child has for her parents. I yearned for his attention and affection. However, his attention and affections were spread hopelessly thin among all his children, his need to provide for his family, and his ever-increasing need for drink. Drink to drown the pain of recurring nightmares resulting from serious emotional battle scars acquired during the war. Nowadays this is known as posttraumatic stress disorder (PTSD), but in those days there was no recognition of this disorder. It was then and is today an unfortunate, invisible, and often lasting emotional and mental affliction for war veterans. Many families had no option but to live with the pain and suffering, often in silence and secrecy, and sometimes in shame depending on the severity of the problem. Some were capable of hiding the symptoms of PTSD, but Father's memories of the traumatic effects of his war experience led him to re-experience symptoms—avoidance symptoms and hyperarousal symptoms. As a young girl I did not know any of this; I simply did not recognize or understand the emotional pain Father was suffering.

My reality became fragmented as I began to seek a safe place in which to hide my own feelings of rejection. I felt lost, as if I were out to sea trying to find the shoreline. My favorite pastime was reading nursery rhymes and fairy tales. Their pseudoreality provided me with hope, the hope of a better life, the hope of security, the hope of happily ever after. As the clarity between what was real and unreal began to blur, everything became patchy, like the quilt that formed the veneer of the island on which we lived. Understanding why my family lived the way we did—with so many secrets—eluded me then. It would only be unveiled later, over time, and pieced together by a master hand far greater than my own.

*   *   *

"Come on, Norma, get away from that window. Let's go do something. We can play checkers. Do you want the white buttons or the black buttons?" said Barbara Ann, the oldest sister. Barbie was always playing the maternal role. She filled in when Mother was either too busy or too preoccupied with what Father might or might not be doing. Barbie always bore the burden for the younger siblings. "I'll get the board," she said, "if you will count out the buttons." We huddled by the furnace grate in the floor to warm ourselves while we set up the homemade cardboard checkerboard. I counted out twelve black and twelve white buttons from Mother's sewing kit. We would barely get our game started when a quarrel broke out. All the other children wanted to play also.

The struggle over who was going to play checkers ended in a playful wrestling and tickling match on the floor. The laundry, which Mother had washed earlier and hung indoors to dry on the rack next to the furnace grate, was knocked over. We began pulling some of the garments over the top of ourselves. "Guess who I am?" one or the other would cry out. And then the guessing game would begin. Little legs would entangle with bigger legs. Arms would wrap around one another as we hid under each garment and under each other. Whoever was "it" would tickle and pinch until a sound came out, and then we would know for sure who it was. This was a game we often played, keeping ourselves occupied as we passed the time.

"You want to go skating?" Mother asked, having just finished scrubbing and waxing the kitchen's tiled floor. "Here," she said. "Put on these wool socks and you can skate all you want."

Pushing the furniture aside, Mother handed each of us an old pair of woolen socks that were either missing a partner or full of holes. This was indeed one easy way for Mother to polish the floor. Slipping on the socks, making sure the holes were on the top part of the foot, we would run and slide across the floor, squealing and laughing, often falling on our bottoms, getting up, running and sliding some more, bumping into one another and knocking each other down.

"This is fun, Mother. I really am skating!" one of us would shout as we got in a good run and a successful slide. We kept up our skating until the floor had a beautiful high-gloss shine. Unfortunately, the shine never lasted long due to little feet tracking in snow and mud throughout the following days. Mother's constant reminder to remove our boots at the door never stuck in our heads, especially while we were in a hurry to be coming and going. Therefore, sweeping the floors after supper became a daily chore for the kids. Taking turns, we often gathered two or three dustpans full of island dirt.

* * *

Darkness fell early on the homestead during those short wintry days. While electricity was available in the 1920s in the larger urban areas of PEI such as Charlottetown, it was not available in rural Prince Edward Island until after the Second World War. Even then, it was not fully available to the majority of rural islanders until after the 1960s. Hence as each winter day wore on, Mother would retrieve the oil lamps from the shelf and clean the glass globes in preparation for the oncoming darkness. We would spend our evenings huddled by the kitchen's woodstove, sitting around the table reading, each of us struggling to glean a share of the lamps' dim light.

Mother stoked the fires in the stove hoping for Father's early return from town, especially when the weather grew threatening. Soon Father would appear with a silly grin on his face, a sack of groceries under his arm, and several pounds of flour and sugar for Mother's constant baking needs.

Saturday night was always a treat: homemade baked beans, hot dogs, and Mother's special homemade crusty bread, fresh from the oven, with just the right amount of butter, molasses, or brown sugar. Mother had spent the day baking several loaves of bread, and the aroma of freshly baked bread was so comforting as it filled the kitchen. We couldn't wait to get the first bite. All of us wanted to have the end piece, which we called the crust, because it had lots of flavor in it. Mother hoped the number of loaves would last the family throughout the upcoming week, especially for school lunches. Cookies and brownies were also baked on Saturdays, but we were not allowed to eat many. These too had to be saved up for school lunches; however, we were allowed to eat one warm oatmeal and raisin cookie as they came out of the oven. This was a special treat for us but causing Mother to have to bake another dozen or so during the week.

Often there was a surprise in Father's grocery bag for the children, usually a block of ice cream, which Father placed in the old icebox to keep cold. Iceboxes were common in many homes before electric refrigerators were invented. In winter months, Father would harvest our constant supply of ice from the frozen pond on the farm. He would store as much as he could in the icehouse outside in the backyard. But inside the home the old icebox had to be replenished every day with ice, because it was constantly melting. In summer months the ice was purchased from an industrial provider. However, the family's need for ice was the last thing on our minds on these Saturday evenings; eating the ice cream before it softened into slush was first and foremost. We couldn't wait to taste it.

Even as children we knew the ice cream was indeed a payoff for the disappointment of not being able to go to the skating rink or on some other adventure that day. But we were so happy to get it; we had already forgiven Father for his misdeeds and enjoyed our treat. To this very day I love to eat soft ice cream because it brings back memories of happier moments sitting in a circle on the floor with my sisters and brothers, giggling and laughing, a bowl between our legs, squirting soft ice cream between our teeth and making milk mustaches.

Each Saturday after supper, Mother would begin the laborious task of filling the tin tub for baths. She retrieved water from the hot water tank on the side of the woodstove, while Father filled more kettles and pots heated on the top of the stove. He retrieved this water from another tank sitting outside the front door. Both of these water tanks had to be filled from the pump house every day. Mother would get us dressed in our boots, coats, scarves, and mittens, give us a couple of buckets, and send us marching out to the pump house to fill the buckets and carry the water back inside. We always followed the path Father had already carved out of the snowdrifts during his daily treks to and from the barn. As children we found the filled buckets to be so heavy we would have to double up, one child on each side of the bucket. If we were in-sync, we would manage to carry the water without spilling or splashing. But if we were out-of-sync with one another, we would often splash the water and get each other wet, creating an argument, "It's all your fault. Can't you be more careful? Why are you being so sloppy?" After we handed the bucket over to Mother to empty into the tank, she would send us back to the pump house again. "This time, try to be more careful," were her unsympathetic instructions. "Then you will not need to make so many trips back and forth." The memory of us struggling to prime the freezing cold pump and to carry buckets of cold water into the house during those winter days is still very painful. However, during the summer months it was not quite as painful, yet the chore still had to be accomplished and the woodstove still had to be fired up in order to heat the water for cooking and baths.

Because there would be several changes of water, bath time was by necessity a concerted effort. Everyone would pitch in. The infant was the first to be bathed, then the next two or three youngest, and so on, until all had received a shampoo and a good scrubbing. Mother would sing, "Rub a dub dub, three kids in the tub," as she passed each child off to Father, who would dry us with a rough towel that had air-dried on the rack or outdoors on the clothesline that very day. Often he would throw the little ones in the air until they giggled and got "overexcited" as Mother would complain. However, she was more afraid Father would drop one, as he was typically a bit tipsy from having spent the afternoon at the Canadian Legion drinking whatever was offered him by his buddies.

As the oldest girls grew into young women, each of us would

demand more privacy. We would request a solo bath in the confines of our bedroom, which meant a basin bath rather than a tub bath. In addition, we would take turns washing each other's hair in the kitchen sink, styling and curling the hair into long ringlets. Finally with pajamas, shiny noses, and the fresh smell of clean hair, we would all sit around the woodstove for story time until bedtime. At other times, we would memorize Bible verses or catechism in order to prepare for that week's Sunday school. When we finished, each of us would line up, oldest to the youngest, to kiss Mother and Father good night.

I can still remember Father yelling up the stairs so we would get quiet and settle down for the night, "If I have to climb this wooden hill, you will all be sorry. I don't want to have to use my belt." There were times when Father did use his belt on one or two of us, just to teach us that we better learn to listen and obey, or else. But Father always made certain that the "smack" with the belt was well deserved by the one or two who might be causing trouble. "You children should be seen and not heard" was another favorite saying of Father, which he reserved for special occasions, when infrequent visitors came to the house, during visits with grandparents, or weekly trips to church.

I smiled as I thought about those outings—outings that were few and far between. It was not often that Mother and Father would take the family anywhere. The effort required to get all ten children ready on time and all to fit into one car was a real challenge. Father would make the eldest of the four children sit across the backseat, and then place the youngest ones between their legs, numbering eight children in all; he and Mother would take the front seat with one little one in the middle and one in Mother's arms for a total of twelve passengers. Every time Father would make a roll call, calling our names, and we would answer excitedly in turn, "Here!" laughing out loud, so happy to be going somewhere.

But that laughter didn't last too long before we would start the normal, riotous "dance" with one another.

"Sit still!"

"Stop wiggling around!"

"You're wrinkling my dress!"

"You're pinching me!"

"Stop jumping!"

"You hit my chin!"

"You spit on me!"

"Oh, your nose is running."

Or anything else we often say that showed our childish and selfish impatience to get to our destination. That is when Father would give his "Father Bear" roar, "Get quiet and behave yourselves or I'll stop the car and put you all out on the side of the road." We actually believed he would do just that, because in such situations, Father was indeed a man of his word, a man of conviction.

Father demonstrated his strong convictions and his love for his family in many subtle, tender, and responsible ways. During the winter, on stormy days when school was not cancelled unless there was a whiteout, Father would place all the children's books and lunches in an old flour sack, sling it over his shoulder, and lead us to the two-room schoolhouse. He would take the path through the woods that sheltered the lot of us from the wind and cold. "Now, you children line up, youngest first and Barbie at the tail end. Make certain you follow in my steps so you will not get lost in the woods."

Following in Father's footsteps was not easy, as his stride was bigger than our little footsteps, but we felt more grown up and important when we managed to keep pace. As we crossed the open fields the wind whipped around, tearing at our hats and scarves; sometimes, when the wind was really strong, we would have a rope to hold between Father at the front and Barbie at the back.

In the middle of the forest, there was always an uncanny silence like being in the eye of a storm. The snow would crunch noisily underfoot, and we could almost hear each other whisper.

Indeed we could hear the trees crackling as the branches rubbed against one another, as if they had their own language, telling each other amazing secrets. I wondered what they might be saying to one another, especially when a tree would shed one of its branches. *Did they mourn the loss of that branch,* I wondered, *the way we mourn the loss of a loved one?*

Occasionally a stray crow would break into the silence with a piercing caw. The lonely sound pierced my heart. I actually felt sorry for that crow even though I knew Mother did not like crows. "Darned old crows," she would often say when they took up residence in her vegetable and fruit gardens during summer months; or even later in life, when they bothered her bird feeders outside her patio doors. Not even a scarecrow seemed to keep them away, and she would end up chasing them with her broom as often as she chased the chickens out of the front yard. But in the loneliness of the snowy cold forest, my heart went out to that "darned old crow."

The fresh fallen snow was the purest white anyone had ever seen. It was a magnificent experience, so magnificent we would want to return to it over and over again. However, Father warned us, "Never ever walk through the woods by yourselves, as it is so easy to get lost."

At other times when the snows were not too deep, Father would hitch up the wooden sleigh that he used to clean the stables. He would arrange bales of hay along the sides for seats, cover it with straw, and let Star, the family's black horse with a white star on her forehead, carry us to school. Father would make each child get underneath a big old buffalo tarp to keep the wind from getting little faces frostbitten, while he himself braved the wind and the cold. Oftentimes if he was not clean-shaven, he would end up having ice particles on his lips, nose, and mustache.

As we climbed in and out of the old wooden sleigh with manure residue on the sides we all held our noses, afraid we would smell like manure all day long. "Father, do we have to sit there?" we would plead. "It stinks!" But Father assured us that it was frozen hard and would not get on us. We were fortunate it did not thaw out as we sat near it.

On sunny days we walked the approximately one-mile trek to the schoolhouse, sometimes hand in hand or two by two, depending on how well we liked each other that day. We ran and skipped as happily as we could through snowdrifts, at times climbing up on the banks piled high by county snow ploughs, often tripping over telephone wires that ran from pole to pole along the roadside. Many families were able to afford the telephone, but we did not have one in our home at that time. From the height of the snow bank, we would shout down to one another, "I'm the king of the mountain and you're the dirty rascal!" Such exhilarating activity on frosty mornings would leave us wide-eyed and rosy-cheeked for the start of the school day.

There were other ways Father showed his love for his family. Many nights the north Atlantic wind would howl through the rafters of the house. The chill in the air was so strong it would freeze the water in the chamber pots underneath our beds, and ice about an inch thick would form on the windows. Father would sit up half the night stoking the coal and wood furnace down in the cellar. Dry heat would rise from the furnace, up through the grate in the floor, and continue to the second floor bedrooms. However, the north wind would defeat the old furnace, unable to produce enough heat despite Father's efforts. I would have to cover my head with blankets or snuggle closer to my little sister in order to keep warm. Often I would see Father walking quietly through the house carrying his lamplight or flicking his cigarette lighter in order to see in the dark. I can still hear the click of the lighter going on and off as he walked about checking on each child, tucking us in under the covers. I watched him while I pretended to sleep. The sense of security I felt in those moments would be so powerful but brief. The next day, I would awaken again to the worries and concerns of daily living. Even for a child, they were heavy indeed.

*   *   *

The stewardess startled me back to reality as she announced over the intercom, "We are making our final approach into Charlottetown. Please extinguish all cigarette smoking, place your seat backs and seat trays in their full and upright position, and make certain your seat belts are securely fastened." I began folding my blanket as the stewardess repeated her instructions in French. I thought of my daily childhood awakenings and this current unexpected awakening by the stewardess. Always, the question would be looming before me. How will I deal with these feelings of loss and insecurity? However, in this situation I knew full well I had lost Father a long time ago. That awareness made my grief harder to bear. Although we had made peace with each other and had an unconditional love for one another, we had never been able to communicate on a deeper level. Now I would have to deal with the loss of a parent-child relationship that could never ever be recovered.

*   *   *

Along with my family, I went through all the motions of attending to and greeting the guests at the wake. I listened to a fairly new minister of our church say some final, empty words. He did not really know Father or his pain. Mourning at the graveside and watching the casket being lowered into the ground, I hoped the undertaker did not find the note I had slipped into Father's pocket. It was a note expressing the many things I had not been able to say directly to him, a note of forgiveness, love, and at least, some partial understanding. I searched for something to hang on to, something significant. Besides this large wonderful family, where was Father's legacy? What did he leave for me that was meaningful and worthy? That was my heart's desire on this day.

The more I thought about it, the more I came to realize that a father's legacy is not always imminently recognizable. Sometimes a legacy is revealed only over time, through memories or through a deeper latent understanding of just who that man truly was. There were several characteristics I held onto, characteristics that were so profound. I remembered his strict parenting skills shaping my convictions of what was right and wrong, good and evil, honorable and noble. I remembered Father teaching us the Golden Rule, "Do unto others as you would have them do unto you," and striving to enforce obedience to the Ten Commandments. As we grew older and more independent, we often failed to remember his guidance, each of us seeking our own set of rules.

I remembered his failures, but I also remembered his persistence and determination. It was precisely these qualities that had helped me through many trials, many disappointments, and struggles of my own. These experiences would eventually make me strong so I could walk through my own fears and failures, to welcome them as a challenge to even greater development.

I remembered Father's desire to seek after God. Every Sunday that he was able, he would take the children to Sunday school and church services in a little white church with a large majestic steeple. It sat on the corner of a crossroads between Malpeque and Darnley, approximately three to four miles from our home. There was a special sense of security, a sense of reverence as we approached its doors. I can still see the local folks walking into that little church from cars parked alongside the road. Each one dressed in their Sunday best. Each one cleaned and polished, freed from the dirt off the farms or the odor off the fishing factory. Each one greeted one another with a warm hello, and each one took what seemed like the same "self-designated" seat every time.

On these Sunday mornings, Mother would invariably run out of time to get herself ready, even if she had something to wear besides an old housedress. She would therefore remain at home. I believe Mother was actually happy for the couple hours of peace and quiet she found as she prepared Sunday dinner. Sometimes I imagine her whispering a little prayer of gratitude for those quiet times. I believe, without a doubt, God honors the sacrifices Mother made on behalf of her family for there were so many.

Father was immensely proud to sing in the choir, along with two of his own brothers and friends from the community. He always sat on the right side of the choir loft so he could get up and pump the organ for the organist when there was no power. Additionally, he loved to watch his children grow within the church family. On special occasions, his five daughters would stand and sing special hymns and praises to everyone's enjoyment. I remember the people telling him what a beautiful family he had and this too made him proud.

Throughout the years, as Father's untreated PTSD symptoms grew and his desire for drink grew, the church was a safe place for Father to understand God's forgiveness. God's unconditional love, grace, and mercy extended to our father through his church family made him feel valued and significant. I will always hold our church family in the highest regard for their love toward Father and our family. Their love and acceptance taught me a lesson—that we, as individuals, should always strive to encourage and to help others reach this place of safety, value, and significance wherein we can all recognize the face of God's love.

As I pondered Father's search for spiritual significance and personal value, I realized this too had become my own search. Now I knew this was indeed Father's legacy and one so powerful it would, over time, weave together all the pieces of my young life that had once been tattered and torn. Father's legacy would serve as an exquisite triumphant inheritance, a divine treasure capable of transforming my heart and leading me toward my own destiny.

For the Lord is good and his love endures forever; his faithfulness continues through all generations.

—Psalm 100:5 (NIV)

The Miracle

Located halfway between the equator and the North Pole in the Atlantic Time Zone, Prince Edward Island experiences a wide range of seasonal changes, all of which are unfailingly beautiful. Spring has its particular magical elements, arriving around the first of April. The deep snows begin to melt and soften the ground. The large icebergs in Malpeque Bay and other inlet bays, along with the gray seals that frolic and sun themselves on these icebergs, depart. Frothy ocean whitecaps that had been hidden by great sheets of ice can be seen rising and falling once again in a comforting rhythm on the horizon. The muddy red soil releases its heavy moisture with help from the spring breezes and the warming sunshine. As leaves begin to emerge on the fruit trees and the apple orchards fill out with blossoms, robins and other flying creatures return to find their ritual nesting places.

After being shut in all winter, the islanders find the burst of activity around the community inescapably contagious. Fishermen load their freshly painted and repaired boats with traps and other gear, anxiously awaiting the imminent start of the lobster season. Each one hopes the season will produce enough income for his family for an entire year.

Farmers, their lives having been slowed to a crawl by the heavy winter weather, begin to plough their fields, leaving trails of dust amidst unspoken prayers for a productive growing season. Barking dogs chase anything that moves, including the farmers on their tractors.

Homeowners, especially those in the tourist industry who have converted their homes to a Bed and Breakfast (B&B), dig deep into rigorous spring-cleaning activities preparing for the hoped-for onslaught of summer tourists.

Shopkeepers daily sweep the entrance to their storefronts

and holler at passersby, enticing them to come see the new merchandise.

Children, having shed their heavy winter coats and boots, run and play with a newly found sense of freedom, excitement, and foolhardiness. Parents and teachers can hardly contain the children and send them outdoors to expend their energy.

I remember my brothers and sisters and me plodding in our rubber boots ankle-deep through the red mud as we walked the long country road to school each spring day. I was one of those rambunctious children who loved the spring season, risk-taking, and adventure. From a young age I had a natural curiosity, running to the top of a hill just to see what was on the other side and somehow knowing that one day, I would travel and see the great world beyond this island.

When the ground dried out, I would lie in the grass and watch the airplanes fly high above, or listen off in the distance to the whistle of the trains that came to the island on ferry boats, and wonder where the people might be going. These ferry boats had train tracks on the lower deck that allowed the trains an off and on access. Often my imagination would carry me to far-off places, as a companion to the travelers, on those same planes, trains, and boats. There was a yearning for adventure in my heart that did not seem to be present in the other children. If so, I never realized it and we never talked about it. If one had asked them, my sisters would say I was not only a natural leader but also I was one who always tried to get my own way. I was also a lover of make-believe, a carefree tomboy climbing trees, hanging upside down and swinging by my knees on the branches, splashing in puddles and making mud pies for dinner in our make-believe house in the forest.

"This is the bedroom and this is the kitchen; that fallen branch is the cupboard," I would tell the other children on forays to my fairy tale house in the woods.

"Let's bake our pies in this oven and set them along here to cool."

"I'll be the wife and you be the husband and all the others can be the children," were my directives.

At other times I would command, "I'll be Sleeping Beauty

and you be the dwarfs. Go out and bring home the food for the day, but pretend you are surprised when you come back and find me sleeping here. One of you will have to be Prince Charming who will kiss me and wake me from my sleep." Yes, I was always casting my vision and the other children would willingly follow my lead, at least until they had their own ideas of what they wanted to do.

As spring progressed into summer, and the wild berry patches began to bloom and produce fruit, Mother would often find us deep into the patches enjoying a luscious snack of strawberries, blueberries, and at other times raspberries. We would have red and blue stains on our tongues and lips as there would be so many delicious sweet berries. Then Mother would bring along little bowls and have us fill them with the sweet rewards from God's bountiful nature. "We'll have these for dessert tonight," she would say. "Perhaps I'll bake a pie." That made us more determined to find as many as we could, often competing with one another to see who could gather the most, and arguing, "Mother, don't you think I have more than my sisters?" Mother would then command us, "Stop arguing and fighting. Enjoy the warm sunshine. Enjoy each other's company and watch out for anthills!" Watching out for anthills full of these stinging little creatures immediately changed our focus and made us very conscientious about what we were doing.

When fresh strawberries reached their peak on Prince Edward Island, it was another good sign for the children. It meant that the ladies in the community would plan their annual Ice Cream Social fundraiser. This was one of our favorite times of the year. In addition to the homemade ice cream with freshly crushed berries, they also offered home-baked pies, cookies, squares, and cakes. It was such a joy to meet with all our friends and neighbors, share stories, and indulge ourselves on these delicious treats. I always chose something with chocolate because these are my favorite. I still recall my brothers, sisters, and me walking along the display table taking a great deal of time choosing which treat we would purchase with our limited spending money, instructed to "mind our manners" or "we would have to go out and sit in the car." Father, who sat at the back of the hall talking with the other men, would keep his eagle eye on us to make certain we obeyed his directives.

*   *   *

One afternoon when I was five, Mother heard terrifying screams coming from the children inside the kitchen.

"Mother, Mother, come quickly! Norma has fallen and is hurt real bad."

"What happened?" Mother asked as she burst into the kitchen to find me lying in the fetal position on the floor, wailing and writhing with pain.

"She was swinging on the door," said Barbie, "when she fell backwards onto this old stool." Barbie explained that I had gotten up onto the old stool that had a broken back, the one Father was always planning to fix but never seemed to get around to it. When the door was open I climbed onto the doorknob, putting one foot on the inside doorknob and another foot on the outside doorknob while holding on to the door as in an embrace. One of the other children would swing the door back and forth to give me a joy ride while I tried to hold on. This was something I had seen the older children do and I thought I was finally big enough to undertake the challenge myself. However, on this occasion, my grip gave way under the momentum of the swinging door. I fell backward onto the broken stool, one of the vertical rungs puncturing my bottom and piercing my colon like a spear.

Mother immediately sensed that I was in deep trouble. She grabbed several towels and gathered me in her arms, barged through the kitchen door, and started running down the lane. Mother yelled back at Barbie to watch the other children until she could return. There was no telephone in our home, Father was away with the car, and Mother was hoping Mr. MacKay, the neighbor who lived across the road, would be home and able to drive us into town to the doctor's office. Mother thought the doctor's office was closer than the hospital, and the doctor could help her discern the seriousness of my accident. Was it as bad as she thought? As Mother ran along, she realized she could go faster if she put me down and then come back for me.

"No, no, please don't leave me here, Mother!" I cried out. But she explained that she would be right back. She needed to run as fast as she could.

Lying on the side of the dirt road, I felt intense pain unlike any I had ever known. Tears were streaming down my face. I was gripped by fear, and I was keenly aware of blood running out of my body. As black flies swarmed around me, it seemed like an eternity before I saw Mother returning.

I will never forget the image of Mother running toward me that day. The island wind was blowing so strongly that Mother's hair was pushed straight up off her forehead, and her lips were stretched taut against her face. Her housedress was caught between her thighs, and her stockings had fallen down around her shoes. Little trails of dust arose with each footstep on the red clay road. It appeared as though she was struggling with the wind as it fought to hold her back, but with clenched fists she kept punching forward until she reached me once again.

Mother scooped me up in her arms and we sat on the side of the road to wait. Mr. MacKay was out in the fields when Mother spoke to Mrs. MacKay, so it would be a few minutes before he could come along with the car. Mother wrapped me tightly in the towels as she held me in the most tenderhearted embrace I had ever felt from my mother, who was not one to spend a lot of time hugging and caressing her children. Soon Mr. MacKay arrived and we were loaded into the car. Mrs. MacKay was dropped off at our home to help eight-year-old Barbie take care of the other children who, at the time, were one, two, four, six, and seven.

Mother kept holding me close, rocking me back and forth in the rear seat. Amidst my pain and fear, I was aware of feeling and loving this special tenderness. Yet in my head I was singing, "Rock a bye baby on the tree top. When the wind blows, the cradle will rock. When the bough breaks the cradle will fall. Down will come baby, cradle and all." In my heart I knew that baby was down.

The next day in the hospital in the little town of Summerside, my body was filled with infection, my temperature was extremely high, I was hallucinating, and my lungs were badly congested. I had what the medical community calls a systemic infection. The hospital staff and the doctors told Mother and Father, "She may not pull through. It will be touch and go." The year was 1956. Penicillin was still not widely available.

However, unbeknownst to Father and Mother, Dr. Zielinski, who had recently moved to our little town of Kensington, was very familiar with penicillin and its reputation as a wonder drug. He had served in the Polish Army and the British Command during the Second World War. He had witnessed the miracle of penicillin used on soldiers after the invasion of Normandy.

The Zielinski family had suffered their own trials. In her memoir, *Poland to P.E.I. Through the War and Four Continents*, Janina, Dr. Zielinski's wife, said, "We were without a home for ten years, and after an experience in Russia in a concentration camp where I lost my father, my sister, my uncle, and my aunt, Prince Edward Island felt like heaven. My husband, who received his doctor's degree in Beirut, Lebanon, got hard labor for eight years in Siberia...."

Years later, I came to believe that the arrival of this family to Prince Edward Island in 1952 and the presence in a small town of a doctor with a keen knowledge of cutting-edge medicine was simply miraculous. If the hand of God had not caused the intersection of these lives, I might well not be alive today.

The memories of my hospital stay remain vague. I can recall a single bright light and many faces looking down on me. Most likely, I realized later, that was the operating room where I was taken for stitches. I recall wrestling with my mind and one hallucination that remains particularly poignant. Dressed in a long white gown I floated through the hospital, up over and above the pediatric cribs, high enough in the air that the tail of my gown was trailing below my feet. It felt as if I was going somewhere, and I distinctly remember waving good-bye to the other children in their hospital cribs. Later in life I would ponder this incident and wonder whether it was indeed a hallucination or something more. I wondered if perhaps I had had a near-death experience but I am not sure, because that is all I can remember.

Whatever it was, I was deeply aware of one thing for certain. The accident had torn the very fabric of my being—something I had never experienced before. I was now acutely aware of guilt, shame, and fear. Guilt because I had done something I should not have done to cause so much trouble; shame because I had to expose myself to so many strangers who touched me where I did not want to be touched; fear because my spirit had lost its sense of freedom, happiness, and joy. Emotionally I was troubled like I had never been before, and I was too young to understand why. There was blackness in my spirit where there had been light.

The power of the guilt and shame enclosed me and overrode any sense of the miracle of healing that was taking place in my body. Even as I made noticeable progress in getting better, I wanted to run and hide.

After a month in the hospital, the doctor instructed Mother and Father, "Make sure she remains quiet at home for a while longer. Her immune system is still weak, so be careful she does not get reinfected."

This would be an impossible task with all the other children at home, so upon leaving the hospital, Mother and Father took me to spend some time with my maternal grandmother, Nanny Stewart. Separation of this kind, away from the ones who loved me the most, was both a refuge and a curse. I gained a sense of relief being away from the other children teasing me for becoming a "crybaby," but the separation also felt like abandonment, driving the guilt, shame, and fear deeper into my spirit.

I had never spent much time with my grandmother. Nanny lived in a farmhouse in the small rural community of Hamilton with her brother, my great uncle Claude, and her son, my uncle Charlie. Lying on the sofa in the kitchen during the day, I kept an eye on my uncle Claude. He was retired and didn't do much of anything except read, sit in his rocking chair looking out the window, watching the vehicles coming and going up and down the road. Occasionally he would get up and wind the clock on the kitchen shelf, a clock that seemed to have the loudest "tick, tock, tick tock." At other times he would let out a grunt or two as if he were trying to say something to me, but I just ignored him and looked the other way. When no one was around, the silence within the room exacerbated both the clock's sound and the creaking of the rockers in his chair, moving back and forth, back and forth on the tile floor. Nanny sat in her big overstuffed rocker in the other room, her sitting room, knitting or reading or doing crossword puzzles. Coming from an active home life, the silence was terribly penetrating. Certainly this scene was not one I, as an active, imaginary child, was accustomed to or felt comfortable being around.

Uncle Charlie took care of the farm, including the foxes, which he raised for additional income. Therefore, he was usually out of the house. At mealtime he would come into the mudroom, wash up, and make his way to the table. He would eat, make limited conversation, tease me a bit to add some meager smiles to the group, and then disappear again. His father, Papa Stewart, being eighteen years older than my grandmother, had died when I was a baby; so being a responsible son, uncle Charlie had taken over the care of the farm and Nanny Stewart.

Nanny was a large woman with a stern face. Because of her size, she was not able to play with the children or come down to our level, so there was a distinct emotional distance between her, as an adult grandparent, and the smaller children. Later, though, as we got older, she became more of a buddy to us. Because Nanny loved to bake bread, pies, cakes, and cookies, we would fight to spend time being her grown-up assistants, especially on Saturday mornings when it was time to bake. My sister Darlene usually won out, as she loved Nanny and actually spent part of her teenage years living with her. However, at the time of the accident, I had not yet developed any kind of personal relationship with my grandmother, who was indeed more like a total stranger.

Because the doctor had instructed the family to keep a close eye on me, especially at night when "her temperature might rise," I remember having to sleep in my grandmother's bed. Nanny could not climb the stairs, so her bed was located in a small room on the main floor. Due to the limited size of the room, the bed was pushed up against the wall. Clinging to the wall so I would not have to snuggle with my stranger grandmother, I cried myself to sleep. I yearned for that loving touch I had felt from Mother on the day of the accident. I felt hopelessly lost and alone.

*   *   *

The old feelings of hopelessness, loss, and loneliness were haunting me on this beautiful spring day as I visited Father's grave for the first time since the funeral back in December. Contributing to my deep sense of loneliness was the fact that my husband of thirteen years and I had recently separated. Now, too, I had my own little girl who was also feeling lost and alone due to the separation of her parents. I realized the responsibility of finding a way out of this newly found hopelessness that gripped me and my daughter was solely mine. There was no road map, no game plan, and no sewing pattern to show me how to pick up the pieces that were falling around me. A deep sense of foreboding came over me and I was not at all sure how I would move forward.

I sat by the gravesite for several hours. As I contemplated my beautiful Prince Edward Island, its wonderful spring season, my younger days, the miracle of my healing at age five and my current circumstances, my thoughts became more prayerful. I wondered about this God, creator of the universe; a God who allowed my father, as broken as he was, to find acceptance and love in a little white church; a God who provides healing to some, as he had done for me when I had that accident, but not always to others. I knew these questions had perplexed even the greatest philosophers throughout time, and I hoped that someday, somehow I would come to understand and know this mysterious, yet apparently, loving God. I knew he had already carried me through many difficult circumstances in life, and that he had even walked alongside of me. I believed that. However, the question remained—did I really know and understand this God? Why did he seem to be with me at times and yet today, so far away? Could I put my faith and trust in him, and how? Just like the unfamiliar relationship I had with my grandmother at age five, there was a division, a level of strangeness that made me want to pull away. I breathed a little prayer asking God to make his presence known to me in a more powerful way, to be with me and to help me make the right decisions.

I reflected backward again and wondered if any adults had prayed for me at the time of my accident. If they had, I was unaware of it. In those days, the Bible was placed on a coffee table in the parlor, and all the children were strictly warned, "Do not touch the Holy Book. Do not tear the pages. Do not write in the pages or get them dirty and wrinkled." The reverence demanded of the Holy Book seemed so prevalent that even adults adhered to this warning. I never saw any adult open the book and bow their head in quiet prayer on my behalf or for any others. No one ever opened the Holy Book that was placed in the pews in the little white church. Why? I wondered. We were taught to recite The Lord's Prayer, Psalm 23, and other verses, but these were handed to us in the form of a catechism. They were not read out of the Holy Book. There was no discussion in our family of miracles or healing or of the power of an omnipotent God. There was just a simple understanding of God's existence and in turn, God's forgiveness, an understanding of what will be, will be.

One thing I clearly remember was Mother and Father teaching the children to kneel by our beds and say a nighttime prayer, "Now I lay me down to sleep. I pray the Lord my soul to keep. If I should die before I wake, I pray the Lord my soul to take. God, bless Mother and Father and all my brothers and sisters.

In Jesus's name, Amen." Often we would add a little personal request such as, "Please help so and so to get better" whenever we knew someone was hurt or ill.

I wondered whether these innocent, heartfelt, simple prayers offered on my behalf by my brothers and sisters had, after all, played a role in the healing that I experienced as a child. Perhaps one of their little voices reached the heart of God. For this thought I felt more hopeful. Remembering Father's legacy, his desire to know God and the little white church I attended as a child, I decided to pray anew, a simple childlike prayer, and ask God if he would be my guide and once again provide another miracle of healing, this time in my heart and more importantly, in my little daughter's broken heart.

The Lord is my Shepherd, I shall not want... He leads me....
He restores.... He guides me....

— (PSALM 23:1–3 (NIV)

THE TRANSFORMATION

Growing up on Prince Edward Island in the 1950s and 1960s had its share of challenges for nearly everyone. In a big family on a farm, each child was expected to "pitch in" and "do their part" of the hard work that was required to sustain us. The daily chores never seemed to get accomplished without a quarrel over whose turn it was to do this or that.

"Work before play" was constantly harped at us, and I learned early that if I wanted to play or read a fairy-tale book, it was best to just get the work done and be free of it. That decision enabled me to become a hard worker. I also learned to work with a sense of excellence and to find pleasure in the work partly because I craved the praises from Mother and Father for a job well done.

Unconsciously I was trying to "earn back" the sense of innocence, wholeness, and goodness I thought I had lost because of the accident. No one bothered to explain that what happened to me was indeed an accident, that there was nothing to be afraid of, nothing to be ashamed of, that Mother and Father would not abandon me again, that it was all right to make a mistake as long as you learn from it. All the reassurances a child needs to overcome the emotional trauma of such a trying experience were simply missing.

Even the old pleasure of going somewhere with my sisters for an overnight visit to Grandmother's, a cousin's, or to swimming lessons in the summer months had become traumatic for me. I became very clingy and would cry to go home every time. Pretty soon my sisters did not want to go anywhere with me because my homesickness would cut short their visit. When they became particularly vocal about their annoyance, I didn't want to go anywhere with them either. No one seemed to understand what was going on in my heart and in my head.

As time went on, I believed if I were really good and worked as hard as I could, then everything would be just fine. I believed Father would abandon his weekend drinking binges that aroused anger in Mother. At a young age, I was learning to carry on my own shoulders the burden of things around me that were unsettled or out of place. I was learning to be a "fixer" and a "pleaser," and I was becoming very good at it.

There was nothing I wouldn't do around the house: sweeping the floors, dusting, tidying up, washing dishes, hanging the laundry outside on the clothesline on Saturday mornings, baking bread, cakes, and cookies with Mother—all the things little girls learn from their mothers I tackled with a vengeance. At the young age of eleven, my sisters—who also learned to work hard—and I had already become accomplished cooks and housekeepers.

I also loved to work on the farm and especially to run freely through the fields skipping and hopping along with the other children and our dog, Rusty. In the warmer months, we would run through the fields to bring the cattle back to the barn for milking. Father would warn the children, "Do not run the cattle.

Walk them back, otherwise they will lose their milk." With Rusty barking at the cattle's heels it was often a challenge, but somehow we managed to accomplish the mission without too much trouble. Sometimes when the cows were drinking from the water trough, we would climb on a cow's back and ride around the barnyard.

Gathering the eggs from the hens was a job I often shared with my little sister, Phyllis. One day we cooked up a scheme to play a monstrous joke on older sister Edie. Edie was the conspicuously feminine one, with long black ringlets and pure white skin. She was always afraid of the animals, especially the hens and roosters, and this opened a pathway for us to tease her. Often Mother defended and protected her, as she understood the fear Edie felt. Yet this day, Phyllis and I convinced Edie to come to the barn to see the baby calf. "It is just so cute!" we said as we enticed her to come along. Edie had no idea what was in store for her. We had opened all the windows to the hen house. As Edie walked past, we shooed all the hens out of their perches and through the windows. Soon they were swarming and squawking over Edie's head, their wings and feet getting caught up in her long curly hair before they came down to the ground. Edie kept screaming and dancing around, swinging her arms in the air and begging for them to stop. Inside the hen house, Phyllis and I were laughing so hard we had to choke back the dust that was flying through the air. We ran outside to torment Edie even more, shouting and taunting her because we felt so proud; we had "gotten her," a really good one. Edie never got over the trauma of the barnyard event; she often brings it up at family affairs, along with other stories, to remind us how devilish we were. Every time we laugh so hard our bellies hurt.

Phyllis was my sidekick. She was petite and loved to tag along with me everywhere I went. Being one year apart, we shared the same bed and almost all our secrets; we were the best of friends. One morning, Phyllis and I overheard Father complain to Mother that there was a skunk coming into the hen house during the night and eating the eggs.

"If only I could catch that skunk or trap it," said Father. "We really need those eggs for our breakfast."

That was all we needed to hear. Together, Phyllis and I made another brilliant plan. We would come home from school that day, wait in the barn for the skunk to appear, and trap it for Father. Easy!

And so we sat for several hours on a bale of straw, eating a snack of homemade bread and butter, telling secrets and day-dreaming about what our lives would be as we got older. Always, our plan was to become a beautiful bride, wife, and mother. We declared how many children we would each have and even chose their names. Using our shirts, we would put a veil on our heads and waltz down the make-believe aisle as a bride, singing, "Here comes the bride, short, fat, and wide." Nothing more came into our minds at age ten and nine, respectively, except I would throw in the idea that I was a beautiful princess who finds my Prince Charming, and we would live happily ever after. We decided we were in the barn today as two Cinderella's who were hiding from our three bossy and very mean older sisters.

Through the window we could see the sun going down and knew that soon Mother would be calling us to supper. It was dusk when Mr. Skunk finally came wandering into the stall and interrupted our lofty thoughts. I had conveniently placed a mallet against the wall near the bale of straw on which we were sitting. We got real quiet, scared, and excited at the same time.

"What are we going to do?" Phyllis whispered.

"Shhh," I said, "Wait till he gets real close. I'm going to hit him with the mallet and knock him out. Don't move!"

Mr. Skunk kept coming closer, as if he were sniffing our scent or the smell of the bread and butter we had eaten. He seemed perfectly unaware of the threat we posed to him. All I could think about was how happy Father would be when we claimed we had captured the pesky skunk.

"Wham!" Mr. Skunk was finished. Or was he? No! He wanted his chance in this battle! He turned around, raised his tail, and sprayed the most awful smell into the air. Both of us were covered in his pungent, concentrated odor. It was just horrible.

Immediately we ran out of the barn and toward the house screaming for Mother to help. No one, not the other children, or even Mother wanted to get close to us. She made us strip off our clothes and climb into the water trough as she pumped fresh very cold water from the pump at the pump house. Someone brought a bar of soap and we scrubbed ourselves raw but to no avail. That smell was not going to leave us.

As it grew darker and colder, we had no other choice but to go inside. Snuggling naked in the corner of the kitchen with a blanket wrapped around us, the odor clung to us as if we had been slathered in baby oil. It permeated the air inside the house. Everyone in the family was angry with us for trying such a stunt. When Father returned home, he was totally surprised at our efforts to rid the henhouse of the skunk, but he did not get angry. After all, he had made several attempts himself at ridding the farm of skunks, and he knew the risk involved. Instead, he went out to the corner grocery store and bought some tomato juice that Mother used to wash our hair and bodies. This did help somewhat, enough for us to go to bed and face the next day. We learned that morning Father had found the skunk we had wrestled with in the barn. It would not be eating any more of our eggs.

The odor travelled with us to school. Again, everyone shunned us. The teacher suggested we sit off from the other children next to an open window. It would be several days before we, and the family, would be free of the skunk odor, but in the meantime, Phyllis and I had learned a hard lesson. Don't fool around with skunks! The children in the two-room schoolhouse learned the same lesson. They thought we were pretty brave trying to capture a skunk but also foolish, and they had a great time teasing us for weeks and months. It would be the following school year before the children at school would forget our heroic efforts to capture a skunk and stop their teasing once and for all.

* * *

I loved school. I had an inquisitive mind and a great desire to learn. Sitting in the two-room schoolhouse that had grades one to four in one room and grades five to eight in another, I learned many new things every day as I listened to the teacher when she taught the higher grades. I was soaking it all in like a sponge.

Each reporting period, I would bring home straight A's and was often recognized by the teachers.

My brothers and sisters did not share the same love of learning and often did not do well in school. On one occasion, Father unwisely said, "Why can't you all be like Norma? She always does her homework and brings home such good grades." I clearly remember the statement causing some jealous looks and eye-rolling amongst the group. At the time, though, I did not care. Once I had overcome my accident and its emotional trauma, I became very competitive. I wanted to excel at everything but for all the wrong reasons. More and more I thought I could change my home situation by being good, pleasing my parents and winning affection.

As I matured, I came to realize that my efforts to create change were not achieving the desired results. Because Father did not receive any treatment for his PTSD, things continued to decline. Father finally gave up farming to take odd jobs during the week. Eventually, he became a school bus driver and custodian for the regional high school. Mother had to take a shift job at the local potato factory where she worked on the product line all night long. This was very hard work for anyone, standing on a product line all night in a cold factory.

I remember waking up on wintry mornings watching Mother come home from work, pull a chair up to the woodstove, and put her feet in the oven to warm them. "Ohhh," she would say, "this feels so good. My feet are as cold as a block of ice." It hurt to see Mother so tired and worn out. She slept during the day when the children were at school. Each of us had to "pitch in" more and more with housekeeping and chores.

Mother continued to be supportive of Father, yet at times she would become angry, and the family continued to keep its secrets. Eventually, all the older girls had to take whatever job we could to bring in a dollar here and there—babysitting, picking potatoes in the fields during harvest, and doing janitorial services at the two-room schoolhouse—whatever was necessary to deal with the poverty we had fallen into.

*   *   *

"Stop pushing your broom so hard, Norma. You're raising too much dust," said Darlene, who was one year older than me. "We'll never get out of here." We were sweeping the floors at the two-room schoolhouse after school. I was not at all happy. I was tired and hungry and wanted to go home, but the amount of red dirt that had been carried in on the schoolchildren's feet that day seemed massive.

"If you create too much dust in the air, it will take longer to settle and longer for us to get the desks and the floor polished. So please slow down," Darlene said again. I was not about to listen to Darlene or any of my sisters, for that matter. They always seemed to be bossing me around and I didn't like it, not one little bit. Furthermore, I did not like having to sweep the schoolhouse or dust the desktops or scrape other children's chewing gum from the underside of the desks. The more I did it, the more I resented this job.

I too was becoming angry with Father for making his children work at such menial jobs. What I didn't notice or care about was that I was supposedly building character. At least that is what Mother assured us we were doing when we complained. She stated so emphatically, "Hard work never hurt anyone!" What I didn't notice either was that there were other families in our farming community who also had a number of children working hard in order to sustain their families. At the time, I thought we were the only ones.

I was reaching the age where being the good little girl was being replaced with a concern for what my friends were thinking. I was also learning there were people, even in a small rural community, who had a better way of life than ours. As my attitude changed, I was growing in self-absorption and selfishness. I wanted what other people had. I wanted things I knew I could not have. I wanted the fairy-tale life that I read about in my fairy-tale books. I wanted a glamorous life. More importantly, I wanted to experience peace, joy, happiness, and contentment in everyday life, without having to live in secrecy and shame. And while it was sensible, even valuable, to wish to fulfill these desires, I did not know that each one often carries its own special price tag—a price I would pay as my fairy-tale dreams became the quantifier for my life and consumed my every thought.

*   *   *

"Mirror, mirror on the wall, who's the fairest one of all?"

My sisters and I were growing up, it seemed, way too quickly. As we primped in the mirror and fussed and fumed over our ill-fitting, unfashionable hand-me-downs, Mother would often say with a raised eyebrow, "Beauty is as beauty does," or "Beauty is only skin deep," and then leave us alone to contemplate what she meant. Mother, who was an extremely beautiful woman herself, had a way of pricking the conscience, that "thing" God had placed inside of each person to help distinguish between right and wrong.

Many times my conscience would hurt when I was feeling particularly good about something in my physical appearance while knowing full well that my heart was not right with its growing resentment and anger toward my father. As my character and personality traits took greater shape, I sensed within myself bewilderment, uncertainty, disorder, and a lack of under-standing. These muddled pieces of my personal development with their frayed edges drove me deeper and deeper into a false reality and further from the divine principles I supposedly had learned in the little white church. I struggled with that inward spirit that wanted to do what was right, according to the voice in my conscience, but often came out thinking, saying, or doing the wrong thing. I believe most teenage girls feel this way as they struggle to reach maturity and to find purpose and meaning to their lives.

Oftentimes I would ask Mother for advice on this or that. Her answer was always, "It's up to you, dear!" without any direc-tion whatsoever. Other times I would ask my older sisters for advice and information. They would answer only, "You are just too young to know. Mother will tell you when the time is right," as if they had some great big secret that in keeping to themselves made them feel powerful. They would go into their room, when the three of them shared a room together, and they would slam the door on me. Because the door didn't shut tight all the way, I tried to peek in on them. I wanted to see how their bodies were changing and why they were being so private. I tried to eavesdrop on their conversations to see what I could learn, but they would chase me away, telling me to "mind my own business." At times they would tell Mother on me and she only reinforced their privacy. This infuriated me, causing me to withdraw even further from my sisters and my parents, leading more and more toward independence and a presumptuous self-reliance that kept me from trusting anyone, adding to the struggle within my conscience. I was smart enough to know there was something more, some knowledge that grown-ups shared, and I wanted to know what it was, but to no avail.

And no matter how hard I primped, and no matter what Mother meant by "Beauty is as beauty does" or "A smile is the prettiest thing we can wear," with my heart in the wrong place I never felt I looked pretty. I recall a time when my sisters and I were together in church. We had just finished singing one of the special music selections for the day. Afterward, one of the neighbors approached Father, tapping me on the head, saying,

"You have such a beautiful family, but I don't know whatever happened to this one. She is so homely." Given my frizzy brown hair, my skinny little boyish body that was slow in developing, and my hardened heart, I believed the statement to be true. This comment by a friend of the family reminded me later in life that adults should always be careful what they say to children, because little ones do take everything to heart.

The truth is I was growing into a beautiful young girl, just like Mother and my sisters, and each of us had a particularly winning smile. My youthful beauty, smile, gifted homemaker skills, shyness, gentleness, and playfulness with children, along with my independent and self-reliant personality, won many accolades for me and, in particular, many babysitting jobs. One summer, at the age of thirteen, I worked for a family at the Air Force base in the little town of Summerside cleaning house, preparing meals, and babysitting an eleven-year-old just a couple years younger than I was! This is just an indication of how fast we matured into responsible young women, able to maintain a household.

* * *

But "being responsible" doesn't always mean "being wise in the ways of the world." It was a stormy night in January. I was going about my regular activities working for the Vaughn family. (Name changed to protect the innocent.)

Since the end of the ninth grade and just barely fifteen, during the summer months I lived in their home to care for the children while the parents were at work. This job continued into the fall and the new school year. During the week, after school I prepared their evening meal, cleaned the kitchen, bathed the children, helped with their homework, and put them to bed. Finally, I would do my own homework and get myself ready for bed in their guest room. The pay for this work helped to offset any expenses my parents had for my school clothing and school supplies, now that I was attending the regional high school. Any additional funds were often shared with the family.

But this night was different. The mother, Mrs. Vaughn, pregnant with another child, went into labor. The weather was particularly threatening with snow, heavy wind gusts, and scant visibility. Mr. Vaughn called the local snow removal team to have a snowplow lead his car through the storm to the hospital, where Mrs. Vaughn gave birth to a girl.

*   *   *

Just like Little Red Riding Hood in the forest, that night I was unaware of the presence of the big bad wolf. I lay sound asleep in my bed when Mr. Vaughn returned from the hospital. He slipped quietly into my room so as not to awaken his young sons. Mr. Vaughn took me that night, destroying my sexual innocence. He convinced me not to tell anyone of this time together. He led me to believe that I was his now, to do with and when as he pleased. He made me believe that this arrangement was completely in keeping with my role in the family. He led me to believe that he loved me, that I was special and precious to him. He made certain that role had all the proper appearances. Mr. and Mrs. Vaughn would be naming their newborn daughter after me, he claimed, and I would become the little girl's godmother. This was his calculating plan.

I now know this deception was evil at its highest and darkest level. I also know that this man targeted me on the school grounds. He came to our home to specifically ask Mother and Father if I could go to work in their home, stating, "We would take very good care of her." Why me? Why did he not ask for one of my other sisters? It's not that I would have wanted my other sisters to go through this ordeal, but as we look back, it is evident that his asking specifically for me was a clear indication that I had been targeted.

I also know now that his deception and targeting became psychological brainwashing. This man knew exactly what he was doing. I was a vulnerable child, shy, prone to secrecy, living a fairy-tale reality, playing "house" with this family, and totally uninformed, uninstructed, and uneducated about anything sexual between a man and a woman. I had no notion, let alone even a vague conception, of abusive behavior by adult men toward children. I was malleable, like putty in this adult man's hands. Over time I was brainwashed into believing that Mr. Vaughn's behavior was normal, yet I had a gnawing feeling that something was terribly wrong. I tried to rationalize my situation. After all, I thought, Mr. Vaughn was Father's friend, and Father had allowed me to go live in Mr. Vaughn's home. And wasn't Father grateful for the income I was bringing home for the family? That was my troubled, continued, naïve way of thinking. In actuality, Father knew nothing of this abuse.

I felt repelled by this new relationship; instinctively and without knowing precisely why, I felt deeply ashamed to tell anyone what was happening. I knew in my conscience that this situation did not fit Mother's words, "Beauty is as beauty does," but I did not know how to get out without revealing my dark secret.

One weekend when I was to go home for a visit, I made up my mind to tell Mother and Father what was happening to me. Unfortunately, when my parents arrived to pick me up, Father had been drinking too much at the Canadian Legion, where he and Mother had spent the evening. He was weaving on the road. Mother was begging him, "Please stop the car and let me drive," but he refused. I spoke up, also trying to convince Father to please let Mother drive the car. Father did stop the car, right in the middle of the street. He turned around in his seat and yelled at me to remain quiet and to mind my own business.

Just then, a blue light and siren came on. Father was arrested for driving while intoxicated and was forced to spend the night in the county jail. As he was taken away, he yelled back at me, "This is all your fault! If you had only been quiet." The incident tore at the seams of my fragile relationship with my father. When he returned home the next day, his silence and despondency clipped any remaining threads of our relationship that were still intact. There was no sense of closeness, nothing, except unspoken anger and contempt in both our hearts. I knew I would not be able to share my secret with Mother and Father this day, nor perhaps any day.

That Sunday, I returned to my job with the Vaughn family and to my growing sense of deep shame. This time I brought with me the additional burden of not knowing where I really belonged. As this new relationship with the Vaughns evolved, entangling me ever more tightly, I pushed my shameful secret further and further inside of me. The child did carry my first name and I did become the baby girl's godmother in a church service where I only felt more shameful in front of God. Soon I grew increasingly more sequestered. I even began to accept my condition as my newfound reality. I convinced myself that I was in love with this man and his family. Believing this was love seemed to make everything all right—it seemed to erase some of the guilt.

Yet I also grew spiritually and emotionally depressed. My interest in school and school activities disappeared. I began to lose weight and receive failing class grades. I felt as though I was caught in a psychological war between right and wrong. Finally, I broke down.

Mother and Father were advised by the high school principal to take me to the office of the family doctor, Dr. Auld. There I wept as I revealed my secret to Dr. Auld and my parents. I was "quietly" removed from the Vaughn household. No charges were pressed, and I was expected to go about my life as though nothing had happened.

Father looked at me as if it were my "own fault," and Mother did not say a word. Now I would have to live with my secret in a new way, not only with a sense of overwhelming guilt and shame, but also with the condemnation I felt from my parents. Soon, I too began to blame and condemn myself for what had happened, thinking I should have known better. I should have stopped those acts perpetrated against me. I should have done this. I should have done that! I questioned myself over and over, *Why, why, why? Why did I allow these things to happen to me? Why didn't I just say no? Why did I allow myself to bond and identify with this family?* I worked myself into a blind frenzy, a whirlwind of self-loathing and doubt. I felt like I was caught up in the tornado like Dorothy in the *Wizard of Oz*, and I desperately wanted to find my way home!

No answers were forthcoming. I would find the answers only years later, in a psychology class at university. I discovered I had been the victim of traumatic bonding, or capture bonding. This is where a victim identifies with her captors. This can happen even when there is not a hostage situation. It is called Stockholm Syndrome.

In his book, *Love and Stockholm Syndrome: The Mystery of Loving an Abuser,* Dr. Joseph M. Carver explains it this way: every syndrome has symptoms or behaviors, and Stockholm Syndrome is no exception. While a clear-cut list has not been established due to varying opinions by researchers and experts, several of these features will be present:

- Positive feelings by the victim toward the abuser/controller
- Negative feelings by the victim toward family, friends, or authorities trying to rescue/support them to win their release
- Support of the abuser's reasons and behaviors
- Positive feelings by the abuser toward the victim
- Supportive behaviors by the victim, at times helping the abuser
- Inability to engage in behaviors that may assist in their release or detachment

I've had many years to think about all these things, particularly in the context of my current work with victims of sex trafficking. My volunteer work and my research confirm that all these features are present in a brainwashing situation. Today I look at a 15 year old girl and I wonder what her level of maturity is. Does she know what she is doing? The answer is no, she does not. This was a question I often asked myself as I reflected on my experience. I knew what I was doing was wrong. However the worst part was feeling the utter powerlessness within the situation.

As the sex trafficking industry has increased in the twenty-first century, a US Federal law was established to protect children. The Trafficking Victims Protection Act (TVPA) of 2000 established that children under the age of eighteen need protection due to their level of immaturity. There is no doubt in my mind that this age level should also apply to children pursued by sexual predators. Any child who has not reached the age of eighteen should never be coerced, persuaded or encouraged to perform a sexual act with someone who is in a position of power or otherwise.

The damage that is done to a young girl by a pedophile affects not only her body but also her mind and her spirit for a long, long time. For a perpetrator to steal a few moments of pleasure from a young victim without any concern to how he affects her life is unconscionable, and nowadays the perpetrators not only victimize a young person for pleasure, they also sell them several times a day to other pedophiles for money. This is a scourge on humanity and especially a scourge on the males who participate in this type of activity. I believe God will harshly punish these perpetrators for their atrocious crimes against his precious innocent children. As a matter of fact, the Holy Book states, "If anyone causes one of these little ones—those who believe in me—to stumble, it would be better for them to have a large millstone hung around their neck and to be drowned in the depths of the sea" (Matthew 18:6, niv). In plain words, God is telling these people who victimize his little children they are better off drowning in the sea than having to face his wrath. Facing God's wrath is very serious business.

My passion today, as an adult, is to bring awareness and prevention to at-risk vulnerable young girls, boys, and their parents; to help others see that these forms of abuse can take place in any situation, including churches and homes, and to be constantly on guard. That is why I am speaking out and sharing my secret. We cannot do enough to protect our children from the exploits of the big bad wolves who seek to devour and destroy our youth in this manner. Unfortunately, at a young age I knew nothing of this kind of abuse and the psychological phenomenon of traumatic bonding until I unwittingly became one of its victims. I wish someone—a teacher, a friend, a coach, a counselor—anyone had made me aware. But back then, we never talked about sexual exploitation. The words were not even a part of our vocabulary.

Nowadays, though, it has become a hot topic as the problem has grown to huge proportions. It is now a multibillion-dollar industry, with more than three hundred thousand children exploited every year in America and millions more around the world. We must all speak up and tell younger children the potential dangers. We never know whose life we might save.

* * *

Unfortunately, for a period of time thereafter I continued to allow my confusion and self-contempt to rule. As I tried to heal and recover from my traumatic experience without any counseling and my parents' silence, I found myself in my own self-made prison. I missed many days of school while I stayed at home to recuperate. Nothing seemed to work for me.

After a time, I sought relief by going to church one Sunday, the little white church with the majestic steeple. I had been avoiding God in both my prayers and my church attendance, thinking that I was not good enough anymore. But that day, I decided to go and meet him directly. I could no longer run and hide from him. I thought that God would hear my prayers better if I met him at his house. I was actually making an appointment with God, showing him I was serious about overcoming my guilt and shame, desperately needing him to help me because nothing else was working for me.

That particular Sunday, the church was offering the sacrament of Communion. I had not taken the classes that would permit me to go forward to receive Communion, but sitting there in my seat, I felt an overwhelming urge to go forward. As I stood, my older sisters tried to stop me, saying, "You haven't taken the membership classes yet, so you're not allowed," again trying to let me know that they had all the answers. But they did not know the need I felt. I ignored their warnings and walked forward.

Standing at the front of the little church, below the altar, I heard the minister say, "This bread symbolizes my body that was broken for you. Eat in remembrance of me." In that instant, I felt overwhelmed by a crystal-clear sense of God's divine presence with me. Then I heard the minister say, "This wine symbolizes my blood that was shed for the forgiveness of your sin. Drink in remembrance of me." As I took the bread and the wine, I wept like never before. I did not know then that no one comes to the Father except by way of Jesus. Yet God, my merciful heavenly

Father, knew this truth, and he not only kept the appointment I had made with him, he invited me in, providing the way for me through the Communion service that was offered that Sunday morning. It was as if he took me and led me by his own precious hand.

In that moment, I knew God had forgiven me. I knew I had been made clean again; I knew he had extended his mercies on my young broken spirit. I felt a strange yet amazing release from the sin, guilt, and shame that had overwhelmed me. I realized I was free again! What a glorious transformation! What beautiful, pure, unadulterated love God extended to me that day. I had never experienced such pure love, and I wanted this transformation, this experience to last forever.

I sought the Lord, and he answered me; he delivered me from all my fears. Those who look to him are radiant; their faces are never covered with shame...The Lord is close to the brokenhearted and saves those who are crushed in spirit.

—(PSALM 34:4–5, 18 (NIV)

THE TRUE VICTORY

The transformation I experienced at the altar that Sunday launched an amazing healing process in my life. I felt a deep sense of communion with God through the natural beauty of my surroundings—landscapes, sunrises and sunsets, the moon and the stars. All of God's creation touched me in a way I never noticed before, giving me an unusual peace and strength as I went about my daily tasks. *There is no doubt,* I thought. *I have found shelter with the Most High God!* In the past, this was a refuge that eluded me in both my home and my community. I relished this new awareness as my mind, body, heart, and soul were being renewed through God's tender embrace, soaking in every aspect of these experiences, filling up every fiber of my being, grateful for his love, grace, and mercy.

I spent most of my free time over the next year playing contentedly with my three younger brothers, Kendall, Rodney, and Scott, and two younger sisters, Rhea and Paula. My companion and friend Phyllis was working at another job. I missed our close relationship, especially our talks. I had not shared my darkest secret with her because I felt so ashamed. Furthermore, I did not want her to judge me, express her disapproval or her lack of understanding. I needed to first reach my own level of understanding.

The beach in the summer months was one of my sanctuaries. Playing in the beauty of our surroundings, I felt safe yet with a somewhat detached, doubtful mind, expecting there to be another major catastrophe in my life.

We would spend many hours gathering seashells, making sand castles, and rolling down the beautiful pink sand dunes that are common to the beaches on Prince Edward Island. Once completely covered in sand and mud, we would go swimming.

"Last one in is a rotten egg!" we would shout running toward the water, diving into the cold surf or splashing each other as we braved the cold. Due to the Gulf Stream that comes into the North Atlantic, Prince Edward Island is actually noted for some of the warmest water temperatures north of Florida. However, as kids we thought it was pretty cold, especially with the ocean breezes cooling the air around us.

Often I reminisce about these wonderful natural healing properties given to me by the Creator. I hear the sound of the children's laughter and the call of the seagulls as they fly high up and dive overhead. I smell the pungent odor of seaweed that lines the beach and the sweat and salt that covers our bodies. I feel the warmth of the water on my feet and ankles as I walk through a tributary where the ocean cuts a path in the sand while making its way toward an inlet pond, and I feel the warmth of the sun on my back and shoulders as well as the soft breezes that caress my skin and tousle my brown curly hair. And I can still feel the miniature silver fish as they swim around my toes or the sting of a

jellyfish on my leg or arm, which have me running and screaming to get away from those menacing sea creatures.

I recall the beautiful sunsets that never cease to amaze me,
recognizing these as God's fingerprints in the sky, his message
of beauty and a foretaste of life ever after. I recall running with a
mason jar to catch fireflies, which seemed like little angels with
wings, and lying in the hay fields looking at the stars. We always
tried to find the Big Dipper and the Little Dipper, the only celes-
tial constellations with which our young minds were familiar, all
the while listening to the crickets and frogs begin their nightly
prayers of praise.

At other times, when the island breezes would die down and
the rhythm of the ocean would find its calm, we would take long
leisurely walks along the shoreline barefooted, shoes in hand,
watching the tides come in and the sun setting as it cast its long
warm glow on the serene waters. Even the ocean seemed to say it
was time to take a rest, relax, and be still.

On Sunday afternoons we would join Father at Cabot Park,
a provincial park where Father served as caretaker during the

summer months. We had the run of the place through the campgrounds greeting the tourists, playing at the beach, and running along the trails. By midday, each of us would take our quarters and other loose change down to the canteen to buy a soda pop, an ice cream cone, or an orange and vanilla creamsicle—my favorite. We earned this money by collecting pop bottles and beer bottles that had been thrown out of vehicles into the ditches along country roads—ditches that were overflowing with beautiful pink, purple, and white lupines that grow wild in summer months—or bottles left behind at abandoned campfires on campgrounds and on beaches. I wondered why the tourists could be so careless as to toss away "money." Did they not take pride in picking up after themselves when they enjoyed our beautiful beaches and countryside? I wanted to tell them, *these are some of the most beautiful beaches in the world. We islanders take pride in our beaches!* Their carelessness didn't make any sense to me. At the same time, though, we were thankful to find these little treasures and cash them in for spending money.

At the canteen, it seemed to take hours making a decision,

asking the cost of this or that item as we struggled to make up our minds, knowing that once the money was gone, there was no more. Soon the decision was reached, and we would sit down on the wooden sidewalk in front of the canteen, side by side, to enjoy our treat. "Can I taste yours?" was the way the conversation would go. Taking turns, we would trade a sip or a taste of each other's purchase, making certain the trade was "fair," not too big or too small. Our youngest brother, Scott, always got away with more than his fair share but that was fine—he was, after all, the baby of the family.

Finally, having received our fill of the sun, the beach, and our treats, we would take long walks on the trails that stretched for miles high along the cliffs of the seashore, singing "Polly Wolly Doodle" or any other tune that came to our minds. On these cliffs the wind would be stronger, making the marram grasses dance to its whistling tunes and to our artless tunes. Out there on the cliffs I could hear the song of the ocean rising and falling, creating its own symphony, sometimes beautiful and sometimes with an eerie lament, but always strongly impressive. I noticed my heart harmonizing with this song from the ocean, sometimes poignantly sweet and other times sounding like a wail. But all the while, I was aware that this was the purging and healing my broken heart needed. It was just the right medicine continuing to echo in my spirit throughout the week.

Before long my ordeal became a distant memory, and I started giving it little thought. However, the trauma and the shame I felt remained with me throughout my life, even though it was tucked far away inside. Every time I thought about it, I would thank God for his forgiveness and push it further away. I recognized that even if there had been counseling available to me at that time, it would not have been nearly as good as the immediate healing I experienced from the hand of the Great Counselor. This filled my heart with gratitude and gave me a renewed sense of value as a young person.

Soon I was able to refocus my attentions on my schoolwork as well as other school activities. I was invited to join the high school marching band and was appointed drum majorette, playing the snare drum during band concerts and leading the band in parades. Dr. Auld, the family doctor with whom I had shared my secret, was an extremely compassionate man. He was responsible for gaining this position for me. Somehow he knew this would be beneficial healing for a young girl who had been through what I had been through. I will never forget this gracious man and his truly inspiring kindness.

The power I felt when I dressed up in the ornate uniform, cape, and hat commanding and leading the band through the streets of many small towns was indescribable. That power became even more exhilarating when, in front of viewing stands, we would be judged on our performance. I would salute the band, swing the baton in a more complicated routine, and signal them to start playing. My heart would skip a beat when the band did well and we received a round of applause from the judges and the audience.

The position of drum majorette further elevated my self-esteem, making me feel I could be the center of something important without being violated. Additionally, the music and the band practices provided a routine that I fully enjoyed—a routine that was apart from the janitorial services our family conducted on the high school property. As we assisted our custodian father, we were learning to dutifully perform these tasks without complaint, a change in attitude from that of our earlier janitorial career. Perhaps we were beginning to understand what Mother meant by her repeated comment, "Hard work never hurt anyone. It builds character," and her comment being continually reinforced by Father's constant repetition, "Work before play." We had learned that whether we complained or not, it was best to go ahead and finish the work so we could move on to other activities.

Before long, I was making new friends. By senior year, I even had a boyfriend named Mack whom I loved and adored. We dreamed and planned about getting married someday, having our own family and our own fairy-tale reality. But this dream was not to be a part of my destiny, as there was another fairy tale in my future, one that had started long before I realized it.

* * *

One afternoon during the earlier recovery process, I was convalescing at home with Mother and Father. Recently the wonder of electricity had reached our rural community, and we were able to afford a black and white television. It was a small TV with a coat hanger for an antenna towering above it, like some twisted artifact, requiring us to jump up time and again throughout a program to make the necessary adjustments for clearer reception. As usual, Mother was sitting in her faux leather recliner with her feet elevated. Father was lying across the broken-down sofa that had been badly beaten and torn by rambunctious children. One leg of the sofa was propped up with old, used schoolbooks. I was sitting at the end of the sofa by Father's feet.

There was no great level of comfort spending this time with my parents. To the contrary, there was still a high level of unspoken tension brought about by continued silence by all. We were watching a rerun of the *Bob Hope USO Tour*. Bob had just introduced Miss World, and she looked absolutely beautiful and radiant in her gown and crown.

As I watched her walk onto the stage, smile, and wave at the troops, out of nowhere I could hear a voice in my head saying, *That's going to be you some day! Hmmm,* I thought, *what's this all about?* At first, my heart did a flip-flop just thinking about the possibility. But hearing the voice seemed neither here nor there.

It was a simple matter of fact that "just happened." Nothing like this had ever happened to me before, and I thought it was merely wishful thinking because of my former trauma, my discomfort sitting there in remorseful contrite silence with my parents, or was it because of my fairy-tale dreams that had become a pseudoreality for me as I sought to escape my hometown life?

Yet while the voice seemed so real, the prediction seemed ludicrous. There was simply no pathway for a farm girl from Prince Edward Island to stand on a stage with someone like Bob Hope. So I ignored the voice and the vision, but for some reason I didn't forget it.

Within a year I was invited by my high school principal to represent the Kensington Lions Club in the local Miss Community Gardens beauty pageant, a part of the annual community harvest festival held each year in the small town of Kensington. The festival drew an audience from all around the wider community.

I willingly accepted the invitation purely as an opportunity to live out my fairy tales, not giving a second thought to the voice in my head and the vision that I would share the stage with Bob Hope. The Miss Community Gardens winner would move on to the provincial pageant and, if successful there, would go to the Miss Canada pageant.

I won the local pageant and was crowned Miss Community Gardens. But that's as far as it went. I entered the Miss PEI pageant but I did not win, mostly because my solo that night left a lot to be desired. The talent portion of this pageant carried high percentage points. I was extremely nervous singing without my four sisters standing alongside of me, as we had always done in church. My chance of going to the national pageant was now beyond my reach. I was disappointed to say the least, but I concentrated on being Miss Community Gardens, thinking, *If this is as far as the fairy tale is going, then I want it to be the best it can be*. And so it was, while it lasted.

My desire to move beyond the cinders and the ashes did not dissipate. I simply changed the path. Unlike any other members of my family to date, I decided to go to college. Should I become a nurse, a teacher, or a secretary? These seemed to be the only opportunities available to young girls on PEI in 1969. Since my goal was to enter the business world, I chose secretarial school and was accepted by the School of Secretarial Sciences at Holland College in Charlottetown, the capital of Prince Edward Island.

Charlottetown has its own significant history, being the place where the founding fathers of Canada met in July 1864 to discuss the formation of the confederation of Canada. The founding fathers chose the name "Dominion of Canada" for the confederation, and July 1 was selected as Dominion Day.

That fall as I moved to this historic city, I realized I had little time to explore the history or make friends. I was dead broke and on a tight budget. A student loan from my hometown bank covered the costs of education. I rented a single bedroom from a couple living near the campus. The rental fee included the evening meal. I grabbed a cup of coffee and a muffin each morning as I walked to my classes and ate lunch in the cafeteria. This scenario was not far from the cinders and ashes as I had hoped, but at least I was on my own, independent for the first time in my life. I poured myself into my studies, almost completing the two-year secretarial program in one year.

*   *   *

But even before I finished classes, events were set in motion that would change the course of my life. Mr. and Mrs. John Bruno, franchise owners of the Miss Dominion of Canada pageant, were exercising their owner's right to seek and identify prospective contestants to represent the respective provinces at the national pageant. This pageant was held each year in Niagara Falls, Ontario, on Dominion Day. Unlike the Miss PEI and Miss Canada pageants, this was not a talent and scholarship competition. Miss Dominion of Canada was purely a beauty pageant.

The Brunos had seen my picture in our local newspaper when I won the Miss Community Gardens. Now they were inviting me to represent Prince Edward Island in their pageant. The scheduled date would be June 4, 1970, just six days before my nineteenth birthday.

Miss Dominion of Canada held the franchise to four international beauty pageants: Miss Universe, Miss World, Miss International, and Queen of the Pacific. Miss Dominion of Canada would go on to represent her country in each of these pageants.

I was both surprised and shocked to receive their invitation. Could this be true? I was being offered an opportunity to go to the Miss World? Had the "voice" I'd heard while sitting on a dilapidated sofa and watching a TV rerun of the *Bob Hope USO Tour*, seeing Miss World for the very first time, been for real? Was God leading me away from my quiet desperation? Was it really possible that God had a purpose and a plan for my life? Was he showing me a way to develop my faith and trust?

I really wanted to go, not just to fulfill my fairy-tale dreams, but also to satisfy a deep yearning to travel and see the world beyond the island shoreline. Selfishly, I saw this as a golden carriage. But there was more—something within me that I could neither describe nor ignore. I was being pulled to accept this invitation, driven and drawn by an invisible obscure yet powerful force that was truly uncanny.

There were a lot of questions, and I was somewhat skeptical that this might not be a legitimate offer. Nevertheless, with Father's permission, I wrote Mr. and Mrs. Bruno that yes, I was pleased to accept their invitation to represent Prince Edward Island. Whatever doubts I had were put to rest when I received a signed and notarized official entry form. It was indeed legitimate. With great eagerness, I completed the application and persuaded Father to sign as guarantor. The date I sent it off is etched in my mind—April 22, 1970.

I didn't have a clue how I could possibly afford to make the long trip from PEI to Niagara Falls, nor how I could afford the proper wardrobe and makeup needed to be a competitor. I asked the Miss Community Gardens pageant officials to sponsor my application and trip. All they could give me was fifty dollars toward the venture. I had one gown that I had made for my high school prom—a white A-line skirt, a pink brocade, sleeveless bodice, and a pink velvet bow tied around the empire waist. It was neither fancy nor special, but it would have to do. I then made a black sleeveless cocktail dress for my introduction onstage. A national swimsuit designer, Catalina, would donate a bathing suit to each contestant. My older sister Edie, who was more accomplished at makeup and who loved to dress up and look beautiful, taught me some makeup tips. She also loaned me some of her makeup and clothing. "I am so excited for you," she shared, "and I hope you win." I could tell that she was genuinely happy and excited for me.

Mother and I made travel reservations on the train that left from the little station in Kensington. She planned to visit her sister, my aunt Doris, in Valleyfield, Quebec, for a week while I went to the pageant festivities. Mother would then join me for the final night. Even Mother was excited to be taking a trip away from home. The visit with her sister would be a great respite for her.

I can't remember how we got the funds for the train ticket, unless I had some money left from my student loan, or perhaps

Mother and Father were able to save up. Perhaps everyone in the family pitched in, or we counted our pennies for a couple of months; regardless, we were packed and ready to go. A representative from the pageant would meet me at Union Station in Toronto, Ontario, and take me to Niagara Falls for the week of pageant festivities.

Father would remain behind with the other children. As I said good-bye to my family, my brothers and sisters wished me well, but they teased me, saying, "You don't have a chance," and, "You'll never win." Deep inside my insecure heart, with its low self-esteem, I believed their tormenting predictions, but that did not quench my desire to participate in this new adventure. However, I also believed they did not really mean their teasing. I felt that any one of our family members would be delighted, happy, and supportive of one another's goals and opportunities.

Father looked at me with a disparaging look and said, "Don't you turn out like Marilyn Monroe!" Great send-off, Father! Great advice! Yet I knew what he was thinking. Because I had not been able to communicate with my father, he did not know about my experience at the altar of our little white church; he did not know how God had walked with me through the days and months of psychological repair and healing; nor did he know about the "voice" I heard, telling me I would share the stage with Bob Hope. No one knew. These were things I had kept to myself.

I wanted to tell Father, "Don't worry, Father, as God is my witness, I will never again let a man hurt me or take advantage of me. As God is my witness, I will walk with honor in obedience to him." But this was a promise I could not say to my father who was still distant, still caught in his own pain, and still demonstrating an unwillingness to communicate. I just went on, driven by my own destiny.

* * *

The pageant director, John Bruno, met me at the train station as agreed. He was a tall, dark, middle-aged man of Italian descent with a nice smile and an officious air. He said that Mrs. Bruno was with the other contestants in Niagara Falls. We were to go to Toronto International Airport to pick up another gal, Susan Flavell, who was flying in from eastern Ontario.

I followed along like a lost puppy, unfamiliar with public transportation, unfamiliar with the city, unfamiliar with four- to six-lane highways, and unfamiliar with big international airports. I was totally awed and overwhelmed by my new experiences. I was quiet and shy, hardly able to speak my name having been taught by my parents "children were to be seen and not heard." I made a very naive effort to carry on a conversation with this stranger.

Nowadays, I would caution parents and young girls to never ever meet a stranger at a train station and follow along to an international airport. This is the ultimate danger for a young girl in today's world of kidnapping, trafficking, and killings. But then, our level of trust for a complete stranger was much higher than it is today with our ever-changing culture.

Soon we reached our destination at the airport and met up with Susan. My first impression was, *Wow! This gal had it all put together.* She was beautifully coordinated and fashionable. Next to her, I felt like a country bumpkin in my homemade clothes. However, I pushed these feelings aside. I wanted to make the best of this opportunity, no matter how inadequate I felt. We talked and laughed, sharing some personal stories on the two-hour trip in the car.

Once we arrived at the Sheraton Brock Hotel in Niagara Falls, where the pageant was headquartered, we fell in line with Mrs. Bruno, chaperones (some of whom were mothers of former winners), and the other contestants. Canada has only ten provinces, but a few of the larger provinces were divided into regional sections, making a total of seventeen contestants. Certainly this is not as large a pageant as the Miss USA, which was the American counterpart until 1997, when the Miss Dominion of Canada franchise owners retired.

*   *   *

Pageant week was a wonderful magical experience for me. Despite my shyness and insecurity, I enjoyed meeting each representative from all the provinces of Canada, and I especially enjoyed Mrs. Bruno with her winning personality and beautiful red hair. She was easy to get along with and took each of the girls under her wing like a mother hen. She readily shared her pageantry knowledge and experience with us, teaching us what we needed to do to present our best on stage and elsewhere in public. The one thing she repeatedly reminded me, until I became fully aware of it, was to stop using the word "some" in my descriptive sentences—a practice common to Islanders—such as, "That is some good," or "That is some nice."

I was particularly affectionate toward everyone, a genuine "Island girl" wanting to enjoy every aspect of pageant week as a once-in-a-lifetime adventure. Having grown up with so many sisters, I related well with each girl. My room became a gathering place for girl talk, giggles, and connecting. One gal, who was also making her own evening gown, was still working on completing it, so I helped with measuring and hand-sewing the hem. She was grateful, and I was more than happy to assist her. We became good friends during the pageant.

One evening when I was taking a bath, I came out of the

bathroom in my robe, a white towel wrapped around my freshly shampooed hair, skin flushed from the warmth of the bath, and found everyone gathered in my room enjoying the usual camaraderie. Suddenly, everyone got very quiet as they all stared at me. I wondered, *What did I do?* One of the girls said, "You have the most beautiful complexion." Later, that same girl told me she believed, in that moment, I was going to be the winner, because of my natural beauty without makeup.

Even though I had that vision and felt this strong motivating force, I was afraid to believe her or to think of myself as the winner. I was afraid of the unknown. Fear gave me such an overwhelming choking sensation. It wrapped around my body like a coiling snake, trying to squeeze the life out of me. My response was to push back hard against it and just take one day at a time.

There was no formal interview scheduled with the pageant judges. We were told they would nevertheless be watching us, conversing with us, perhaps acting as a waitress, a chaperone, a guest at a luncheon or dinner. Or they might be in a park or on a guided tour with us. We would, however, meet them at the final evening of competition. This style of judging was particularly unnerving yet exciting, as it kept all of us on our best behavior. I believed it would reveal each contestant's true character traits.

My strongest personality traits were displayed one afternoon when we all played baseball in the park. I love sports and was able to "show off" my rugged athletic attributes, being a natural and competitive outdoor girl. The many years of baseball played with my brothers and sisters in the apple orchard on summer evenings and on the playground of our two-room schoolhouse really paid off. I was the star player! It was refreshing to have the opportunity to be the country girl that I truly was as we played and picnicked in the park that day.

Whatever impressed the judges, I was unaware of it. However, the night before the pageant finals, I had another premonition. That night, my mother arrived having been picked up at the train station in Toronto by one of the volunteers. We shared the same room. As we slept, I awoke from a dream.

"Mother," I said, "I just had a dream, and it seemed so real. In the dream I win the title tomorrow evening, but I just don't feel that I will be chosen above all these other girls. I am so afraid."

Mother dismissed my anxiety by saying, "It is just a dream. Don't put too much stock in it. Try to go back to sleep." However, the dream was hauntingly real, and I could not sleep, fearful of what would really happen the next evening now that I was finally beginning to believe and anticipate the fulfillment of the "voice in my head." That vision had carried me along this far in some amazing ways, yet when I surrendered my thoughts and my dreams to it, it scared me to death.

*   *   *

Pageant day brought considerable excitement. Every girl was visiting with her family and friends arriving for the big night. The Miss Dominion of Canada pageant was held in the large ballroom at the Sheraton Brock Hotel. It was not televised, we were told, due to its location in Niagara Falls where it was difficult to generate a clear broadcast signal. Later, I came to believe that the pageant was not televised because it did not have the necessary support and funding for prime time TV. Regardless, every one of us had butterflies in our bellies as the time for our stage presentations drew near.

Backstage, we busied ourselves setting up our personal spaces, lining up our outfits in the order they would be needed on stage, getting our hair and makeup done by professional makeup artists familiar with theatrical makeup.

"I don't like wearing all this makeup," I complained to the artist when she was placing false lashes on my eyes. "It looks so unnatural. I feel like a dance-hall girl or even worse. Can you please tone it down?" I begged. "The worst part is this red lipstick!"

But she insisted by saying, "You will wash out under the bright lights if you don't wear this makeup. You need this so the judges can see your face, your eyes, and your lips. Also, it is needed for the photographs that will be taken. Everyone is wearing this much makeup." Eventually I gave in, realizing I was not being given a choice.

As the starting time approached, we all hugged excitedly and wished one another good luck. The first presentation was the introduction of contestants, followed by the swimwear competition. My homemade black cocktail dress looked great on stage, and I felt I was as well dressed a competitor as any of the other girls.

However, the swimwear competition was my most difficult segment. I literally hated being half naked in front of all these people. As I pulled on the suit behind the curtain, my mind wandered to the official Catalina photo shoot taken by the pool earlier that week. In the group photo, I was able to hide behind the other girls with a towel wrapped around my legs, at least until I was asked to remove the towel.

I wish I could go out on the stage with a towel tonight, I thought, but the snap of my chaperone's fingers took that thought right out of my head.

"It's time to go. Hurry, hurry," she said as she rushed me back in line.

Each segment was followed by professional entertainment for the audience. As I slipped into my evening gown, I could hear the singers onstage. They were quite good, with a booming and powerful tempo. You could tell they were building excitement, setting the tone for the finale that would soon be taking place.

I took a deep breath. Oh my, it will soon be over, yet I don't want it to end. My pulse began to race to the tempo of the music while I stood in line, ready to enter the stage in my homemade prom dress. I could hear Mother's words echoing, "Hold your head high. Don't you ever be ashamed of anything. You are as good as anyone else, and don't you forget it!"

These were words Mother often spoke to each of us girls as we were growing up. And so I did! I obeyed her directives, probably for the first time in my life! I put on my best smile. I lifted my chin, squared my shoulders in military style, as Father had always instructed the children, "Hold your chin up and put those shoulders back!" Then I started walking proud and tall down the runway, with both parents' voices echoing in my head, while the master of ceremonies read my personal bio, which was simple indeed, matching the simplicity of my gown. In that moment, I was not ashamed of anything.

Finally, the time came when the top five finalists were named. Being named one of the top five heightened my anxiety and fear. Behind stage, I was crying. The pageant director, Bruno, came into the backstage, noticed my tears, and told one of the chaperones, "Straighten that girl up. She has to go back on stage." These curt words did cause me to stop crying and prepare for the next phase of competition, the top five evening gown competition, and the onstage interview.

As I entered the stage once again, I thought, *Wow, I feel as though I have been airlifted from reality, as if I am going through this process in slow motion. I feel as though I have entered the dream I had last night.*

Now I gave no consideration to my homemade gown; all my fears and insecurities were lost in these few moments in time. The top winners were being named from the five finalists; second runner-up was Susan Flavell from eastern Ontario, the gal we had met at the airport on the day of my arrival; the first runner-up was Shayne Dion from Calgary, Alberta. Both were older and more mature than me. Both were much more sophisticated and experienced than me. Both were more edu-cated than me, having attended university. As I stood there with the other remaining two gals, we looked at each other wondering who would be selected.

My insecurities were saying it would not be me, but the "voice" was saying, *It is going to be you.* It seemed as though there was a spiritual battle in my mind. It seemed as though time was standing still. I could actually hear my heart pound-ing in my chest. Surely, everyone can hear my heart pounding. The few seconds of waiting seemed like an eternity. Then they announced the winner of the Miss Dominion of Canada 1970 was Norma Joyce Hickey, from Darnley, Prince Edward Island.

Oh my gosh, that is me! Am I really the new Miss Dominion of Canada?

I could hardly believe it was real. Did they really call my name? The voice and the vision, oh my gosh, it really did hap-pen. It really did happen!

Where's my mom? Oh, I wish my father and my whole family

were here! I wish my boyfriend were here. Mack was the one who had encouraged and believed in me the most.

I was given my sash, my trophy, and an armful of red roses. Then I had to walk. My legs trembled and felt weak as I attempted to make my way down the runway. I couldn't see for the tears in my eyes and the lights as cameras from the many local newspaper reporters and others were constantly flashing. But I did make it and returned to take my seat on the chair that was designated for the winner.

This was indeed a dream come true. Only God could have orchestrated the fulfillment of such a beautiful dream. This was his vision and he had guided me, supernaturally providing every step of the way all that I needed to reach this moment. My heart soared with gratitude.

Shayne Dion from Calgary, Alberta, first runner-up; Norma Joyce Hickey from Darnley, Prince Edward Island, Miss Dominion of Canada 1970; Susan Flavell from Eastern Ontario, second runner-up.

Soon my mother was ushered on stage. She leaned over and kissed my cheek and said, "I knew you were going to win." The kiss on the cheek and this vote of confidence uttered from my mother's lips caused me to snap back to reality. Her affirming words were the most precious I had ever heard from my mother. I wanted to take and hold her in my arms, squeeze her, and say, *Thank you, thank you, Mother. I love you so much*, but I didn't do it. There is nothing more a child yearns for in life than to hear affirming words from her parents. Today as I think back to that moment, the words to the famous song, "One Moment in Time" by Whitney Houston floods my heart and mind. It was a moment when "I was racing with destiny" and my dreams had just been realized! Yes, wrapped within my mother's words and her kiss on the cheek was the moment I felt I was more than I ever thought I could be. I realized in that moment this was the true victory. I will remember and cherish her words in my heart—always, always.

Mother and Me

Around midnight, I called my family at home to tell them I had won the title, and I was now Miss Dominion of Canada.

My brother Kendall, who answered the call and who was always a tease, thought I was kidding; however, when Father came on the line, he believed me and shared the news with the rest of the family. I told them that the local newspaper reporters might visit with them at the farm the next day and to be prepared. I also told them that my homecoming would be delayed about six to eight weeks, as I was required to make some other appearances first to Expo '70 in Japan and to the Miss Universe pageant. This was a lot of information for us to absorb at once. The excitement was overwhelming.

I tried to envision the dust this news would stir up for our little community of Darnley and the larger community of Kensington, for the island itself. Surely, the large amount of dust that is raised on the red-clay country roads would not begin to compare with this exciting news. This news would be a surprise to the islanders. Many of them were unaware of my invitation to represent Prince Edward Island. It had not made the news beforehand.

*   *   *

The grand homecoming was finally scheduled six weeks after the big night. It was everything any young girl could have wished for. My community truly honored me in a way that touched my heart beyond words. To be able to have my community pay tribute to me was so emotionally charged. To have the Lieutenant Governor J. George MacKay invite me to the Government House in Charlottetown and then escort me to the dinner/dance that was held in my honor was truly humbling. To have the premier and first lady of our province, Alex B. Campbell and Mrs. Campbell, attend the dinner and sit at the head table with me was also humbling. As the local newspaper the *Journal Pioneer* stated, "The list of dignitaries attending the dinner read like the blue book of the island." And to receive gifts from several of the local retailers was more than I ever dreamed of or hoped for. I was extremely grateful to all.

Everyone beamed with much excitement and pride as the comments made by each of the speakers were beyond any words I had ever heard. Even the members of parliament in whose district our small community of Darnley was located were pleased to take credit and ownership of this new victory. Premier Alex B. Campbell was proud to exclaim, "Norma will be a goodwill ambassador for Prince Edward Island." Already, the expectations were high; already, the pedestal was being built; already, I was feeling overwhelmed by the burden of these well-intentioned and hopeful expectations. While they scared me to death, I continued to smile and carry on, beaming with ecstasy, warmed to the core by this amazing joy! Deep inside I was hoping and promising myself, *Yes, I can and I will strive to fulfill the dreams and expectations these wonderful people have of me, their new 'Island Girl.' I will keep this promise to honor all of them as they honor me. Little did I know how difficult it would be!*

*Left to right: Premier Alex B. Campbell, Mrs. McKay, and Mr. Robert
Schurman, MLA and master of ceremonies, me and Lieutenant Governor J.
George MacKay at a special honorary welcoming home dinner*

Lieutenant Governor J. George MacKay escorting me at the Miss Dominion of Canada welcoming home ball

Around 9:30 p.m. we arrived at the Miss Dominion of Canada ball, where more than four hundred people gathered to welcome me. I was on the dance floor celebrating, dancing with one partner after another. It seemed as if every one in the community wanted to dance with me that evening. I felt like Cinderella at the ball in my new white gown and tiara, and I was enjoying every moment as if I were in another one of my fabulous dreams. And one more unexpected victory occurred that evening. This was a victory that none of the dignitaries or anyone else knew about. It was a private victory between me and Father.

I looked across the room. Standing there watching me with a look of admiration and pride on his face was Father. We just studied each other, not saying a word. Then, graciously and very tenderly, he nodded his head and pursed his lips as if to say, *Well done*. I was elated with joy as I walked across the room and asked Father if he would please dance with me. As we embraced each other in the dance position, I knew this was another precious moment in time. We were both winners! My father and I had won peace with each other, and Father had won the pride and respect of the community.

It would be many years later before I realized why God gave me the "voice" and the "vision" while sitting in hypercritical, self-condemnation on an old sofa between my sullen parents. It was never about winning a national beauty pageant or sharing the stage with Bob Hope. It was always about God blessing me, giving me these heart victories from both my mother and my father.

Without a doubt, it was always about God restoring and rewarding the quiet suffering and brokenness of a young girl.

Heart victories such as these are the true gold, the true meaning of life. Often it takes time for us to realize the beauty of these blessings and the pure treasure that lies within each one. Often it takes maturity and a higher level of wisdom and understanding that is not present in a younger mind. Nothing can surpass these glorious victories or ever take their place. They are more precious to me today than winning the title or anything money or fame can ever buy. My prayer is that every person has an opportunity to come to know and experience beautiful glorious

heart victories, at least once in a lifetime.

Proud parents
Charles and Marion Hickey relishing heart victories with daughter Norma
Joyce Hickey, Miss Dominion of Canada 1970

Whether you turn to the right or to the left, your ears will

hear a voice behind you, saying, 'This is the way; walk in it.'

—ISAIAH 30:21 (NIV)

The Fairy Tale

From the beginning, life as Miss Dominion of Canada was truly a dramatic change. I was suddenly and immediately living a real-life fairy tale. My dreams had come true. Mrs. Bruno played the role of fairy godmother, waving her magic wand and orchestrating a flurry of activities to propel me forward into this new role—shopping, professional makeup training for use on the road, onstage, and on camera, modeling stances and training for use onstage and at the pageants, professional photography sessions for an official head shot photo, passport application, and travel arrangements.

"I love these shopping sprees," I confessed to her, all the while trying not to overindulge or appear greedy yet really wishing I could buy one of everything. Never before had I been able to shop on an unlimited budget. Never before had I been able to visit such large department stores. Never before had I seen so many pretty things from which to choose.

A favorite purchase was my very own set of cherry-red faux leather Samsonite suitcases. They were eye-catching pieces with a black band around the middle and red satin lining inside each case.

These pieces are "some" beautiful, I thought, running my hand over the satin lining. I pledged I would take extra care packing my new wardrobe, lingerie, shoes, and makeup in these pieces! "I'm really going to have a blast with all this travel," I confessed to Mrs. Bruno as she showed me all the tricks of packing to the best advantage.

Another favorite purchase was choosing a store-bought evening gown for the Miss Universe competition. What joy! "Oh, my goodness," I whispered. "I feel like Cinderella getting ready for the ball. There are just so many choices, so many gorgeous gowns!" I couldn't help myself as I ran with delight up and down the display aisle selecting the gowns I would try. "I think I'll choose this one," I finally declared. It was a white sleeveless, bare shoulder gown with a high neckline, an empire waistline with floral trim around the bodice and an A-line skirt. It was simple yet elegant and suited my personality.

And shoes, wow! Bata Shoes International, a sponsor for the Miss Dominion of Canada, gave me my pick of shoes and boots for a whole year. Indeed, this indulgence has remained with me, because the first thing I do whenever I can is shop for shoes.

I didn't find glass slippers, but I did discover a pair of white knee-high patent leather boots. I would be wearing these boots with my national costume during the international pageant's segment called the Parade of Nations. My costume was a rendition of a royal Canadian mounted police (RCMP) uniform. It consisted of the white boots, a royal blue glitter miniskirt, a red glitter jacket with gold military buttons, white leather gloves, and an authentic RCMP Stetson-style "Mountie" hat recognized around the world as a symbol of Canada.

Ear piercing was another new and enjoyable adventure. I

chose a pair of pearl studs. Pearl is my birthstone. I just knew I was going to feel like a princess waking up each morning in my beautiful bed with these precious gems in my ears coupled with the scent of Miss Dior, a pure, elegant, jasmine fragrance that I chose as my signature perfume. Just like Sleeping Beauty, I thought. Yes, indeed this is a real-life fairy tale, and I am just waking up to the reality of it.

Father was flown in from Prince Edward Island to Toronto to spend a weekend with Mother and me. We had to sign some contracts for my participation in the international pageants. Within two weeks of winning the title, I was joining fifty-six of the sixty-four Miss Universe delegates in Los Angeles and continuing on to Osaka, Japan, for a goodwill trip to Expo '70, the 1970 World's Fair. Needless to say, there was a lot of traveling to do and a lot to learn in a short period of time. How does a barely nineteen-year-old girl leave a small farming and fishing community and become a world traveler and an ambassador for her country overnight without any training?

* * *

My mind was on information overload during these first few weeks. I was terrified at leaving the Brunos' safe haven, my host home for the year, to travel by myself. The Brunos did not accompany me as chaperones because I would meet my chaperones at each destination. So off I went with my "idiot sheet" containing clear directions on what to do and where to go.

Mr. Bruno said, "As long as you have a tongue in your mouth and your idiot sheet, you will be fine. Just ask for help. The airline stewardesses are there to assist you."

I had never been on an airplane, and my first flight was from Toronto to Los Angeles and then on to Tokyo, Japan! This was certainly my golden carriage, a Pan American 747 flight across the Pacific Ocean. In 1970, Pan Am was one of the leading airlines in the industry, being a launch customer of the Boeing 747 in January that same year. Can you imagine it? One of my first flights and I was flying in a "wide body" only a few months old? Oh, my gosh! It feels like a huge building taking off into the sky!

As I sat in my seat and looked around, spatially it felt similar to sitting on a bale of hay in the loft of our three-story barn—very,

very large. As children, we were greatly familiar with that space as we shifted the bales to suit our make-believe playhouses, or created fabulous obstacle courses. Starting at the height of the rafters of the third story, we would stack the bales on different levels. Then, running and jumping through the course, we would end by flying through an open shaft from the second level to the first level and landing on a pile of soft straw. Father used this straw for bedding the cattle in their stalls, spreading it around with a pitchfork, which was often left lying close to the pile of straw (unbeknownst to us, in a dangerous upright position), not conducive to a soft landing for our two-story flight.

As we took off on this particular 747 flight, I wondered what unknown danger might be lurking around us. Was it as bad as an upright pitchfork hiding in a pile of soft straw? I tried to imagine the power of the engines as we rumbled and rolled down the runway. Everything shook. The thought occurred to me that it might not get up in the air. I grasped hold of the arms on my seat and held on. It just seemed so very, very heavy. But we did rise, and we were flying across the Pacific Ocean with the industry's leading cabin crew. Unlike airline travel today, this crew was serving us drinks, snacks, and some excellent airline cuisine. They were even wearing white gloves, smiling and being gracious—a very personal touch.

No longer did I have to wonder as I did when I was a little girl lying in the grass looking up, watching airplanes flying overhead and imagining where all the people might be going. No, indeed, on this day I did not need to wonder or imagine. I was now, miraculously, one of those passengers. This new revelation made me smile as I straightened up just a little taller in my seat and thanked the stewardess for the meal she was serving me. The experience was better than I had even imagined or hoped for.

* * *

I was absolutely delighted to be in Japan, a land and a people so foreign to me. I learned to say "Hai, hai," which meant "yes," and "*Nipponjenwa totemo sutekedesu*," which meant "Japanese people are friendly." They seemed to like hearing these things. I loved being able to connect with the people of a foreign country, so I repeated these phrases over and over. I was fascinated by the humble gentle submission of the Japanese women as they walked about in their kimonos and slippers, especially the servant maids in the hotels and restaurants. Each time anyone thanked them or expressed a comment, they would bow their head several times, put their hands together as in a prayer, and at times you could hear them giggle, probably because they could not understand a word we were saying.

Riding on the Shinkansen, the "Bullet Train," was another thrill. All the delegates rode from Tokyo to Osaka and back again—another golden carriage; it was shaped like an oblong silver bullet with a circular glass ceiling where you could sit and view everything around you. The train could go as fast as 186 mph and was certainly much more thrilling and modern than riding the tractor on the farm at haymaking or potato-picking time. I never realized such a train existed; it was very much unlike the traditional, diesel-engine train Mother and I rode to Toronto when we went to the pageant in Niagara Falls.

While in Osaka, the delegates would be participating in the

Queen of the Expo '70 Contest held just for Expo '70. "Don't worry," we were told, "this contest is not a true representation of the Miss Universe since all the delegates are not present, and the winner of this contest may or may not be the winner of the Miss Universe. This is a contest established primarily as a futuristic 'expo' experiment because it is actually being judged by computers and not by human judges." Certainly, this was an interesting and novel use of computers at the time because nowadays, judging of reality TV shows is being conducted by computers and smart phones.

Following Osaka, all the delegates and chaperones would travel on another Pan Am flight from Tokyo to New York City with a stopover in Fairbanks, Alaska. We would spend a few days in New York City and finally continue on to Miami Beach, Florida, for the Miss Universe Pageant on July 11, 1970, at the Miami Beach Auditorium. There we would meet the famous singer and heartthrob of the times, Tom Jones. We were all filled with great anticipation.

Spending several hours on a long overseas flight does give

one a clearer perspective on the selfishness of the human personality. I watched as some of the delegates whined in their foreign languages to the interpreters, for attention and service. I watched as some of them drank too much alcohol or wine, getting sick and throwing up on another person. I watched as some flirted with other passengers on this 747 airliner. It was indeed a lesson in how not to behave while representing one's country.

The organizational skills required by the chaperones to move so many people at one time, most with different language requirements and different needs, amazed me. Some of the delegates were cooperative, and some were difficult to manage. Some of them lost their luggage or left their favorite teddy bear behind, anything to make the job of chaperone more difficult, it seemed. I was reminded of the same skills my parents developed moving our big family from one location to another, and I smiled when the chaperones called out our names, this time by country, and we would answer, "Here!"

Just like at home, I thought.

These new and interesting experiences were occurring on

an almost daily basis, like the return flight through Fairbanks, Alaska, witnessing a land where the sun hardly sets; a stopover in New York City, the "Big Apple," a city that never sleeps; seeing yellow and black taxi cabs honk and rush around, bold and aggressive like the "yellow jackets" on our farm, flying in a side-to-side pattern while looking for a place to land; and sitting up, late at night, in the hotel room enthralled by the amazing number of twinkling lights, wondering where all these people were going, what they might be doing, and why they did not think it wise to go to sleep. Seeing the hustle and bustle of so many people who seemed to have a particular purpose in mind was incredibly stimulating. Never before had I witnessed or felt such energy. I immediately fell in love with this dynamic vitality, this exuberant world force. I felt suddenly addicted, wanting to experience more and more.

The unfamiliar sounds and smells of the cities I visited were most unlike the call of the seagulls and the fresh smell of salt air and seaweed on ocean breezes. Even my taste buds had to adjust to inland processed foods unlike the fresh garden fruits and vegetables and homemade jams, jellies, and pickles or the farm-raised beef, pork, and chicken, and fresh seafood and lobster, my favorite, with which I had grown up. I loved trying new gourmet dishes, as if my taste buds were taking an adventure all on their own.

I'll never forget one experience sitting in a fine dining restaurant with all the Miss Universe contestants. I ordered chicken cordon bleu, something I had never eaten before. Watching what everyone else was doing, I copied, trying to pick up the right fork or spoon. We never had this much silverware on our table at home. We were lucky if we had one spoon or fork at our place. Wearing a beautiful beige dress, one of my new purchases, I took my fork and knife to cut into the chicken. As soon as I pierced the chicken, the juices from inside the breast burst forth all over the front of my new dress. I was totally humiliated. This was indeed one of my most embarrassing moments, while the waiters tried unsuccessfully to out the stains with soda water. Unfortunately, I had to spend the entire evening with stains all over the front of me. Needless to say, it was a quick lesson in being cautious piercing a juicy serving of chicken or beef. All these occurrences were creating lasting and impressionable memories for me.

* * *

My arrival in Miami Beach, Florida, in July was shocking. I will never forget stepping off the plane into the heat and humidity of the Sunshine State. It felt as though I had entered an extremely warm oven or sauna, and it took by breath away. This climatic change was more than my Canadian body, especially my feet, could handle. Because we were required to perform many hours of daily onstage rehearsals for the televised portion of the pageant, in our high heels; to walk through the hot public squares to meet and greet local people curious to see the pageant delegates, in our high heels; to make public relations photographs outdoors around pools and hotel patios, in our high heels—my feet gradually became blistered from the unusual heat penetrating my shoes. Even the humidity was having a field day with my naturally curly hair, making it appear frizzy and horrid, or so I thought. However, once I received the treatment I needed, for both my feet and my hair, I was able to focus on the more exciting aspects of pageant week.

My roommate Deborah Shelton, Miss USA, was from Virginia. I was excited to be rooming with Debbie because everyone thought she would be the winner of the Miss Universe. She was indeed a stunning woman with long straight brunette hair that reached her waist, and she appeared to be intelligent and friendly. Being three years older than I was, she also seemed to be more experienced in the ways of the world. All the delegates, themselves considered her the potential winner, "the one impossible to beat."

While we were in New York City at the New York Hilton, she visited each room, welcoming all the delegates to the United States, warning us about the heat and humidity in Miami Beach, telling us, "Don't worry about wearing makeup. It will only melt and run off your face in the heat." We all laughed envisioning the "mess" we would be with makeup running down our cheeks. That would certainly not be ideal for the photographers.

However, my anticipation of having fun girl time with my

roommate was soon dashed. Once we settled into a beautiful suite at the Carriage House on Collins Avenue in Miami Beach, Debbie and I did not connect. We were like *The Country Mouse and the City Mouse*. We did not fit into the same lot in life. The suite was a two-story with two double beds and a bath on the upper level, where I hung out, and a kitchenette and living room on the main floor with a sleeper sofa, where Debbie hung out. Our chaperone was next door. When we were not attending rehearsals and other required duties, Debbie was spending her free time with her parents, who were in Miami Beach for the activities, or with her boyfriend.

Truly, there was little time for us to be pals, even if she wanted to. It was so evident that she was extremely focused on two things, winning and her boyfriend. We were like two ships passing in the night. And I, who had no family or friends attending the pageant, would spend my free time enthralled by the amazing views of Biscayne Bay and the Atlantic Ocean, people watching vacationers enjoying resort-style life and listening to music from my new gift, an eight-track tape player.

As I stood on the second floor balcony of this fabulous hotel overlooking the magical scenery below, feeling the warm evening breezes off the ocean, hearing the music in the background, pondering my new life and its many experiences, there were times when a haunting overwhelming sense of loneliness tugged at my heart. A deep yearning for some semblance of familiarity would overtake me. This yearning for familiarity is a normal condition of the human heart, I would learn later in life.

In these moments, I wished I had someone with whom I could share my new experiences and the unbelievable wonder and joy I often felt. I wished my little sister Phyllis was there, as she and I had always played make-believe princesses. In reality, playing the part without her didn't feel just right. I felt as though I had abandoned her, left her behind, and it didn't seem fair.

My mind floated back to the farm and the family sitting around the dinner table, Mother at one end, Father at the other, and three to four children on either side, on long wooden benches. My two older sisters Barbie and Edie had already left home, both married to their teenage sweethearts, so three of us were missing from the nest. However, it was common for our family to gather at home on Sunday afternoons to reconnect with each other and to enjoy one of Mother's home-cooked dinners. Today was Sunday, which made the loneliness particularly poignant.

I missed Mother's Salisbury steak with mashed potatoes and gravy, or her ham and potato scallops. There was hardly a meal at our home that did not include homegrown PEI potatoes, a staple for a large family. I was also remembering Father smacking our fingers when we tried to be greedy, grabbing food from the center of the table. Sometimes we would play with him, pretending to grab at the food, just to see how quick his response might be, and then giggling if he missed making the connection. "Up high, down low, too bad, too slow," we would tease. These warm thoughts brought temporary reprieve from the moments of loneliness I felt there on the balcony.

At this point, I had not yet made my homecoming trip to the island since winning the title. So I wondered, *Is my family thinking of me? Are they wondering where I might be or what I might be doing?* Later on, I would learn that the local newspaper, the *Journal Pioneer*, was keeping the folks back home well informed of my comings and goings. I learned they were indeed very proud of their hometown "Island girl," and that I had an amazing following. This came to life for me when I started receiving several telegrams from my family, friends, and organizations on the island, wishing me well in the Miss Universe pageant. These good wishes made me feel less alone and served me well, like a lifeline in the sea of inexperience. Even today, I have retained a copy of each and every telegram within my box of memories, sometimes taking them out and reading each one with care, remembering with fondness the person or organization who took the time to send their good wishes. Needless to say, e-mails, Facebook, texting, and Twitter were not available in those days.

Norma Joyce Hickey, Miss Dominion of Canada 1970 with roommate Deborah Shelton, Miss USA 1970 and Libia Lopez, Miss Mexico 1970 at the Miss Universe

* * *

The televised portion of the Miss Universe was the grand finale to this tremendous adventure. Standing on stage under the bright lights, listening to the excitement and the calls of the production team, was phenomenal. The rehearsals paid off. Even with all the language barriers among the several non-English speaking contestants, everything came together in a timely fashion to meet the demands of the broadcaster, CBS. As a contestant in this worldwide pageant, I was feeling like a pawn on a chessboard, being moved here and there with some semblance of meaning.

How are the judges going to make any sense of all this? How are they going to select the top fifteen semifinalists out of sixty-four contestants as we march in the Parade of Nations? It is all happening too quickly! There is no way they can truly select a girl with good character as she marches around the stage for five minutes, or do they really care? Is it just subjective random selection? Certainly, it seems that way. *Beauty is in the eye of the beholder*, I thought, as I confirmed my own thinking. Perhaps it is just subjective selection.

Our interview portion was keenly disappointing. All the delegates lined up at specific times in an outer room. The judges were seated at individual tables in an inner room. We were asked to go in, sit at one table and communicate with one judge, then after a set time, move to the next table and speak to each judge until we had made the rounds. There was no way we could have any kind of intimate conversation with each judge. The time was too short. Needless to say, I was not prepared or taught how to make a quick and witty first impression. I was still very quiet and shy.

You get a sense in a contest like this whether or not you are noticed as a potential winner or finalist. I had hopes that the famous Canadian photographer Yousuf Karsh, one of the judges, might favor me as a finalist, just because we were both Canadians. Even a local Floridian newspaper headlined, "PEI Queen Stands Out," acknowledging the connection with the Canadian judge. However, this was simply speculative thinking by both me and the reporter. I knew in my heart that I was not favored due to my youthfulness and lack of sophistication, yet I participated with a good attitude hoping to be an honorable ambassador for my country.

Bob Barker was master of ceremonies, and June Lockhart was a commentator. I was very familiar with Bob Barker, since *The Price Is Right* was one of our family's favorite programs. From the moment we were able to purchase a television, Mother watched this show every time it came on the air. Additionally, our family was familiar with June Lockhart's roles in the shows *Lassie and Petticoat Junction*. It was indeed a delight to meet these two well-known television personalities and to write a letter to Mother telling her about these special opportunities. Mother, of course, was elated by my news.

When Bob Barker announced the fifteen semifinalists, the remaining contestants were required to "fill in" the stage as background decorations, applauding and cheering the semifinalists. We also performed a well-rehearsed musical number, a song-and-dance routine between sets. It was easy to be supportive even though there was a twinge of envy, not jealousy, in my heart. I felt certain that all the other delegates who had not been selected as semifinalists shared this feeling, but no one said anything. We just smiled and carried on.

I can say the one and only thing I accomplished at the Miss Universe pageant was to have a quote in the local newspaper the *Park City Daily News*, in response to a survey question—which is the most popular skirt length—mini, midi, or maxi? My response, "The midi looks horrible. And I wouldn't be able to walk in the streets with a maxi." To my chagrin, this quote can still be seen on the computer nowadays. Later, as I read my response, it seemed so obtuse, unrefined to me. Yet even today, I believe the most complimentary and classic skirt length on any woman is right at the knee.

Soon the top five were announced: Miss Argentina fourth runner-up, Miss Japan third runner-up, Miss Australia second runner-up. Miss Puerto Rico and my roommate, Miss USA, were left on stage, standing together hand in hand. We were all certain Debbie was the winner.

"The first runner-up is Miss USA, Deborah Shelton, and the new Miss Universe 1970 is Miss Puerto Rico, Marisol Malaret," announced Bob Barker. Everyone was shocked and surprised.

Even Marisol herself was surprised to be the new Miss Universe, yet the truth is Marisol had won the hearts of the judges with her amazing smile and bubbly personality. Perhaps the judges are able to capture the character and personality of the girls after all, I concluded. This awareness gave me some consolation, and I felt very happy for Marisol.

Debbie would go on to become a model and movie star, making many appearances in magazines, including a cover for the March 1974 *Playboy*, and television shows. One of her more famous roles was playing the mistress of J. R. Ewing, Mandy Winger, on the long-running TV show *Dallas*.

For me, I had a whole year of guest appearances as Miss Dominion of Canada all across Canada and the United States, and three more international pageants in which to compete. My fairy tale was not over yet.

* * *

It is very difficult to describe the heavy demands of my schedule during the year, other than to say it was horrendous, yet it was educational and thrilling at the same time. I was assigned to appear, speak, model, do television interviews, ride in parades, cut ribbons at grand openings, and crown many beauty queens at local and regional fairs throughout Canada and the United States. Each assignment required that I look my best, because at every destination I would be greeted with an armful of red roses, festival officials, and local press reporters. Every locale was excited about their particular function and the arrival of Miss Dominion of Canada. It was often their single "big" event of the year. These people did not realize that I had been to several of these events within just a week or a month. I couldn't let my weariness show. Soon all the faces, places, smiles, and stories whirled together like one big merry-go-round and before long, I ran out of time to even journal my memories.

During many small town festivals, I was asked to visit a senior citizen's residence or a children's ward in a hospital. It was during these visits that I felt the most authentic connectedness with people. It was there that I could express my true self and feel the natural compassion of my spirit flow toward those who were elderly, sick, and hurting. This special connection stayed with me afterward as I remembered the happiness and joy my appearance brought to the sick and elderly. Subconsciously, I was beginning to realize that the make-believe, fairy-tale world I was living in was indeed surreal. However, my conscience was maintaining its silence because I was enjoying the newfound fame and bright lights within the fairy tale. I was not yet ready to awaken from this dream or yield to reality.

*　*　*

Among the honorary appearances that are particularly memorable was having my name placed on the cornerstone of a newly built high school in Western Canada as a representative of the Canadian youth; making an appearance and having lunch with Prime Minister John Diefenbaker, the former leader of our country; and making a public appearance with Phyllis George, 1971 Miss America, a delightful representative of her country and a woman for whom I came to have tremendous respect. She was beautiful, intelligent, and talented with a great deal of class, and she was genuinely kind—a true role model for any young woman. Phyllis would later become a cohost of the *NFL Today* as one of the nation's first female sportscasters. She married the governor of Kentucky, John Y. Brown, Jr., authored several books, and worked for numerous entrepreneurial organizations and philanthropic events.

Another prestigious award was being named to the Honorable Order of Kentucky Colonels on April 21, 1971, by then Governor Louie B. Nunn during a visit to Kentucky. At the time, I did not understand the value of this award, and I am afraid the award went into a cardboard box along with all the other gifts I received. Yet today, as I review the mission statement and creed of this order, I am doubly honored: "A Kentucky Colonel is unwavering in his or her devotion to faith, family, fellowman and country; Passionate about being compassionate; Proud, yet humble; A leader who is not ashamed to follow; Gentle but strong in will and commitment." To think that strangers from another country saw these traits in me and bestowed this honor on me is truly humbling. I regret that I went on with my life without acknowledging the value of this appointment.

Additional honors included being given a key to several Canadian and American cities by mayors and being asked on occasion to fly over certain cities, including Toronto, while doing commentary with the morning traffic reporter. Further, while on a jaunt between New York and Toronto, I received an invitation from a stranger to become a face model for Elizabeth Arden cosmetics. I was so naïve I didn't even know anything about Elizabeth Arden Cosmetics, didn't realize it was a highly sought-after line of cosmetics. Instead of taking this man's business card to my manager, Mr. Bruno, I simply refused the invitation because I could not discern whether he was flirting with me or making a genuine offer. Over the years, I have often wondered what my life would have been like if I had indeed become a face model for Elizabeth Arden, but no longer does this question tear at the fabric of my personal identity.

My appearances were typically scheduled back-to-back with

an overnight or long weekend at the Brunos, long enough to do laundry and repack for the next venture. Visits to my family on PEI were few and far between. Whenever I could find time to rest, I would close my eyes and catch ninety winks. One of the places I would often sleep was on an airplane. Like Pavlov's dog that started salivating when he heard a bell ring, I would fall asleep as soon as I heard the click of the buckle on my seat belt, often having to be awakened by the stewardess at a destination point. I was becoming a well-seasoned traveler.

* * *

On October 5, 1970, at 2:00 a.m., a man unbeknownst to me, the British trade commissioner James Richard Cross, was kidnapped at his diplomatic residence in Montreal, Quebec, Canada, by militants of the Front de Liberation du Quebec (FLQ). He was held for two months while the militants attempted to negotiate with the government of Quebec on certain demands, including an exchange of political prisoners. This event in Quebec, which affected all of Canada, was referred to as the October Crisis, and the kidnapping, along with other kidnappings and murders, caused then Prime Minister Pierre Elliott Trudeau to enact the War Measures Act. Civil liberties were suspended and many people were arrested and questioned.

The October Crisis set the tone for my visit to London, England, in November 1970 as the Canadian delegate to the Miss World pageant. My manager and the Miss World pageant officials Mr. and Mrs. Eric Morley felt it was in my best interest to have a private security guard from Scotland Yard assigned to me at all times. They were afraid that someone from England might try to kidnap me in exchange for Mr. Cross.

At the time, I was totally unaware of any potential danger and was not informed about the protection detail. Upon arrival in London, I was told that the security guards were there for the protection of all the delegates; but as time wore on, I wondered why one seemed to be particularly close to me, especially when one day, as I was shopping in the lingerie department at Harrods Department Store, I looked up and saw one so close by. Certainly I also wondered why a guard would sit outside my room at night on a hard chair in the hallway, close to the exit stairwell; yet I still did not make the connection to a probable kidnapping.

On the other hand, my interests were far from any lurking dangers. I was at the Miss World pageant! Engelbert Humperdinck was coming to visit the delegates at our hotel. We were going to see Tony Bennett live in concert at the London Palladium. We would see Buckingham Palace and the Crown Jewels in the Tower of London. We would visit Scotland Yard and later see the famous Clydesdale horses. There were many exciting plans to keep my mind off any potential danger. But more importantly, I was going to meet Bob Hope! My vision of sharing the stage with Bob Hope would soon be realized. There was no need to fear.

The pending visit of Engelbert Humperdinck made all the girls giddy with excitement. We waited anxiously in a large salon of our hotel for his arrival. Some of the girls desperately wanted to be recognized by him. One European delegate was so desperate she came into the salon wearing a see-through blouse with nothing on under the blouse. The chaperones immediately sent her back to her room to "dress properly." But Engelbert's visit did not thrill me as it did the others. Even though I enjoyed meeting this heartthrob, I realized I am not much of a hero worshipper.

However, I was enthralled at the London Palladium listening to Tony Bennett perform. This was my first theatrical experience. The intimate theater setting, the lights, and the music all created magic for me. I fell in love with Tony when he sang "I Left My Heart in San Francisco." And then he sang "Have I Told You Lately That I Love You." I felt totally consumed by his performance. With every "you" he sang, it felt as though he was embracing me! I believe each female audience member felt the same as I did because this was just Mr. Bennett's exceptional, remarkable style.

*　*　*

While civil liberties were suspended in Quebec, Canada, women's liberation activists were planning a protest of the Miss World pageant at Royal Albert Hall on November 20, the final evening. Fifty-eight countries were represented. Outside the hall as people were arriving, a bomb exploded underneath a BBC van as activists tried to prevent the show from being televised. The Angry Brigade, a small British militant group dedicated to protesting American involvement in the Vietnam War, was credited with the bombing. Furthermore, the attendees arriving outside the Hall were being bombarded with demonstrators holding up placards.

When Bob Hope was introduced onstage he tried to joke about the demonstration, but the demonstrators had moved inside. As he joked they started shouting, blowing whistles, waving placards, and throwing homemade stink bombs, ink bombs, and smoke bombs, doing everything in their power to disturb the event, calling it a cattle market, yelling that the delegates were being manipulated and exploited as sex objects. Bob Hope was obviously disturbed by these advances and the show fell into disarray.

To add fuel to the fire, there was great public outcry because the country of South Africa was given permission by pageant officials to send two contestants this year—a black girl Miss

Africa South, and a white girl Miss South Africa. Some stated that this compromise was really in support of Apartheid, and they were quite displeased. To top it off, the winner of the Miss World, Jennifer Hosten from Grenada, was a black girl, and the first runner-up, Pearl Jansen, was the black girl from Africa South. The public outcry of racism by the officials was stunning, and one of the judges, the Prime Minister of Grenada, was accused of persuading the other judges on the panel to vote for his country's representative. Everyone favored Miss Sweden as the potential winner. However, she had made some derogatory public comments about the pageant being a "cattle market," and this may have hurt her. To the chagrin of the pageant, Julia Morley resigned as pageant director. After the voting scores were actually released for public scrutiny, Mrs. Morley was reinstated.

To say the least, the pageant's grand finale was not as anticipated. My time with Bob Hope was far from what I had hoped. My vision, a few years earlier, sitting on the dilapidated old sofa with my parents, hearing a voice tell me that I would share the stage with Bob Hope, had finally been realized, but it was not a perfect outcome. The realization was far from the anticipation I had felt over these weeks and months since winning the title. I had anticipated feelings of great joy in realizing this part of the vision, but there was none of that. Hadn't this been where God was leading me, drawing me into his purpose and plan for my life? I didn't know what I really expected; perhaps, deep down, I thought I was actually going to win and go on the USO Tour with Bob Hope? Didn't the London bookies give me good odds to win? At least that's what some of the newspapers were saying. Wasn't there supposed to be a great connection or the beginning of something more? Yet Bob Hope didn't even realize I existed. I was just another "country" represented on the stage. I did not even get a chance to say hello to him or shake his hand. I was totally devastated. The joy in being there was completely lost.

The pageant and Hope's announcements of finalists occurred amidst total disruption. Only the top five were presented on stage. There was so much confusion the *Associated Press* mistakenly announced in the newspapers that I had been selected one of the top seven. My security guard, who saw me off to the airport the next day, confirmed these statements and I believed him, thinking he had seen the scorecards or had talked with the judges. For a number of years afterward, for some unknown reason, this myth so salved my wounded ego and lent something meaningful to the empty vision that I believed it to be true. I even shared with others that I was a semifinalist at the Miss World showing off the newspaper clipping stating that I had been selected in the top seven. But this belief was shattered with the advent of the computer. One day, I actually looked up the results of the Miss World 1970 finalists and semifinalists and found that what I had believed for years was simply unfounded.

Additional solace was having the memory of conversing with one of the judges, Omar Sharif famous for his role in the movie *Dr. Zhivago, at the Coronation Ball* following the pageant finals. I will never forget his intense, piercing eyes. Oh yes, "Somewhere My Love" still echoes in my head. I was also meeting and communicating with another judge, the famous movie actress Joan Collins, and dancing with another judge, Kenny Rogers, the famous country music star. All these memories did indeed help to compensate for the broken vision that, in retrospect, faded as quickly as one of the beautiful sunsets over Prince Edward Island but without the same glorious penetrating pleasure.

Norma Joyce Hickey, Miss Dominion of Canada 1970 at Miss World in London, England (1st row, 8th from left)

*   *   *

Long Beach, California was the host city for the Miss International pageant held on May 26, 1971, at the Long Beach Municipal Auditorium, my third international pageant, with fifty representatives from around the world.

I was learning things about international competitions that

were puzzling to me. Some of the contestants were enhancing themselves beyond makeup with false hair extensions, breast enhancements, tummy tucks, or plastic surgery on their noses or lips.

Why is this allowed? It seems to me that the contestants should be judged on their natural beauty. It just doesn't seem right or fair, I thought as I began to get acquainted with my fellow competitors. Soon it became a mind game for me to see which one "did" and which one "did not" have such enhancements, while at the same time realizing I had no particular influence over whether such enhancements should or should not be allowed. Yet my questions and concerns still remain unanswered. Nowadays when there is so much controversy over athletes using performance-enhancing drugs and being fined or dismissed from competition because of it, shouldn't similar rules apply to beauty pageants? I believe contestants today should be very outspoken about this topic. After all, not every contestant has the opportunity to afford such enhancements. If it continues to be allowed in beauty competitions, then contestants should in all fairness be required to disclose this information with a before-and-after photo to the judges. However, when I was a young girl, I remained silent. I was incapable of such discussions.

At the Miss International, we would be visiting Disneyland in Anaheim, California, and the RMS Queen Mary that had been moored in Long Beach Harbor since 1967. Both of these adventures raised excitement for me, not yet twenty years old and still thinking of myself as a farm girl from a small community in Prince Edward Island. Who doesn't want to go to Disneyland? I thought, *All my brothers and sisters will be jealous. I must bring them some mementoes from Walt Disneyland. What a great opportunity to take home some special gifts to the younger ones.* And so I did. I not only brought home some special gifts, I also brought home a semifinalist win from the Miss International, which was another jewel in the crown of this Island girl.

*   *   *

I recall one visit to my hometown, running into my high school English teacher. He said, "How exciting it is for you,

Norma, to be able to do so much traveling." He added, "I will never forget your English papers, writing about your desire to travel to see and to learn about the world. You are truly realizing your dream." Hearing my teacher say these things made me feel even more blessed to be able to live out this fairy tale.

But something deeper was stirring inside of me, something I could not yet put my finger on. I was not finding or cherishing a sense of belonging within the fairy tale. This was not the place my heart could call "home."

I remember standing behind the curtain on stage at the Miss International, waiting to be introduced, when a rhyme came to mind. It was as though my conscience was not being silenced any longer. The rhyme went like this: "I have a little shadow that goes in and out with me and what can be the use of it is more than I can see. It sometimes springs up taller than an Indian rubber ball, and it sometimes gets so little that there's none of it at all." A perfect metaphor for my ego as it sprung up taller by thoughts of being special. And also a perfect metaphor for my self-confidence that seemed to shrink to nothing at all as the struggle within my spirit was growing more pronounced. My inner turmoil was getting louder and louder the longer I stayed within the fairy tale.

Being selected a semifinalist in the Miss International pageant contributed to this growing confusion between ego and self-doubt. The selection boosted my ego causing me to think, *Oh yes, I really am somebody special!* Being offered a screen test in Hollywood while at the Miss International further boosted my ego and complicated my thinking. Pride was running rampant, making me stick out my chest and hold my head a little higher.

Yet my father's voice echoing in my head, "Don't you turn out like Marilyn Monroe," together with my lack of trust in men who try to take advantage of young girls, added to my spiritual and emotional struggle, causing fear and forcing me to turn down any offers of a screen test. I felt as though I was navigating between two choices, the glitz and glamour of the entertainment world and the unrelenting "need" within my spirit to do something more meaningful with my life. The temptation to stay within the "fame and the bright lights" was amazingly strong.

It was May, the eleventh hour. My year as Miss Dominion of Canada would be coming to an end on July 1. Soon the clock would strike midnight, and some other young lady would magically appear within the fairy tale to take my place. This hardly fits the promise of "living happily ever after." Something was woefully wrong.

On board the RMS Queen Mary, Norma Joyce Hickey, Miss Dominion of Canada 1970 in her national costume, along with Jacqueline Lee Jochims, Miss USA 1971 and fourth runner-up at the Miss International Pageant 1971

* * *

Following the Miss International, I realized I needed to make some decisions about my future. Time was running out. I recall making another appearance at a local fair. This appearance was a deciding moment for me.

As I pulled up to the hotel where I would be staying, I looked out the window of the car and there on the marquis were these words, "Welcome, Miss Dominion of Canada." I realized my name was not on the marquis, just the title. Suddenly, it became very apparent to me that I was not "somebody special" after all. The truth is that I was being used as a marketing tool for someone else's benefit. The truth slapped me in the face. Its realization was very painful, like a dagger to my heart. In no way had this kind of deception been part of the fairy tales I read as a little girl. These thoughts were very disconcerting to say the least. Yet I needed to face this truth.

Others were making money off my appearances, and I was getting a cut. The harder I worked, the more money everyone made. Furthermore, my contract stated that if I accept a position in modeling, television, or on stage that is a direct result of having won Miss Dominion of Canada, then I would be responsible for giving my manager twenty-five percent of my earnings for the life of the position or career. Even though I felt the franchise owners deserved a percentage cut, because after all they were the ones who had given me this opportunity, I did not feel comfortable with this arrangement. I valued my independence.

As hard as it was to face, it was indeed the answer to the struggle within my spirit. The fairy tale was not the true deliverance to a life of happily ever after! *Oh, what to do?* I pondered.

Still other matters were complicating my thinking. During my visits to Prince Edward Island, I knew beyond a doubt that I could never go back home again to live. It wasn't that I didn't want to. Rather, I realized I could not live up to the expectations the local people had put on me. Some were asking me to be a schoolteacher to impart to children all my experience and supposed newly found wisdom. Some were asking me to become a local TV news reporter; others were asking me to promote the island's tourism. And yes, some were criticizing me, saying that I had grown egotistical and proud. Those in the last group had no understanding of what I had been through as I struggled to figure out how one is supposed to act when there have been drastic changes to one's circumstances. These momentous changes were forcing me to face the longstanding existential questions, "Who am I?" "Where do I belong?" and "What is my purpose in life?" These people did not know how to offer grace; these were the ones who tear other people down in order to make themselves look better.

The sad fact was that rather than being egotistical and proud, I was more than ever a lost little girl. Yet I was wise enough to know that this pedestal the local people had put me on was way too high. I knew that one mistake or one fall from the pedestal offered nothing but devastation. In my spirit, I knew I did not have the strength to face any type of ridicule, especially from those who had loved and honored me. Neither did I wish to face their disappointment. I believe that no one is able to consistently live up to another's exalted expectations. It was better for me to walk away.

* * *

I will never forget the day I walked away from my home. I boarded the plane in Charlottetown, at the time a very small airport with one or two gates. There was no security in the airports like we have today. My parents, who had brought me to the airport, were allowed to stand outside in a gated area, along with other folks who were saying good-bye to their loved ones. As the plane taxied the runway and took off, I could look out the window and see my parents waving good-bye. And then it struck me—this overwhelming sense of solitary isolation, this overwhelming, piercing feeling in my heart of deserted, forlorn abandonment. I began to weep. I wept like I had never wept before. The stewardess on the flight tried to console me but to no avail. I wept the entire two-hour flight from Charlottetown to Toronto. I stopped crying long enough to get to my pickup point and back to the Brunos' home, and then I wept in my bed all night long. I did not know there could be such grief, and no one could help me. Even though I had wished for, even pursued a real-life fairy tale, the cost of achieving it was very, very dear. I had lost my home and myself. "Humpty Dumpty sat on the wall. Humpty Dumpty had a great fall. All the king's horses and all the king's men couldn't put Humpty Dumpty together again." Like Humpty Dumpty, I realized I had taken the fall. How would I ever be put back together again?

I went about mourning as though for my friend or brother. I bowed my head in grief as though weeping for my mother.

—PSALM 35:14

I am worn out from my groaning. All night long I flood my bed with weeping and drench my couch with tears.

—PSALM 6:6

...but his favor lasts a lifetime; weeping may stay for the night, but rejoicing comes in the morning.

—PSALM 30:5 (NIV)

THE CHOICE

As I faced the loss of my personal identity and my home life, I sought the advice and counsel of my friend and mentor Frances Bruno. Our conversations were deep and provocative. I shared with her my inability to find "belonging" in the fairy tale.

"I cannot find true, genuine meaning in the bright lights or a sense that this is 'home,' yet part of me wants to stay within the fairy tale. Is something wrong with me?" I asked.

"Not at all," she assured me. "What you are feeling is actually quite normal. Many of the past winners have also been conflicted when it comes time to choosing a future endeavor."

In addition, I shared my belief that I could not live in my hometown again, not wanting to live under the whispers nor face the scrutiny of my friends, relatives, and neighbors. I would always be wondering if I could measure up to their expectations, wondering if I had their approval, wondering if they could see the real me beyond the package, more worthy than a pretty face, a "beauty queen."

I told my friend and mentor, "I need a safe place where my spirit feels at home."

She asked me penetrating questions such as, "What pleases you the most? Where do you feel a sense of belonging? Do you have a passion for something that stirs you? Do you want to build upon your secretarial studies and go into the business world? Would you like to enter the modeling or fashion world?"

We talked about my deep sense of compassion for the elderly and sick and how my visits to the hospitals and nursing homes stirred something pure and real within me. As we pondered all these options, she suggested I apply to nursing school and see if I could be accepted for admission in the fall of 1971. I did apply and was accepted to the renowned St. Joseph's School of Nursing in Hamilton, Ontario. This school was close to the Brunos' home, and I was happy for the chance to stay nearby my friend and mentor.

Yet there was still great uncertainty about this choice. After what I had experienced during the past year, would this be enough for me? Would I miss the excitement, the travel that I loved so much? My spirit was still in conflict.

As the time grew closer to July 1, 1971, and the realization that I would be giving up my position and title, I grew even more anxious. There was still something within me that wanted it all. I believe this is common to the human condition, to desire that special recognition, fame, and fortune, to desire the accolades and the admiration, no matter how we get it. In a world where everything seems to be changing so quickly, I believe this desire for special recognition has remained constant and basic to the human condition. It has even grown in importance and stature.

I see it in our current culture. Many people young and old are constantly striving for beauty, brains, and talent in order to achieve that higher level of recognition and respect; are driven by ambition and success; are constantly comparing themselves to other people; are continually measuring personal worthiness by job titles, the size of homes, the type of automobiles, and the brand of clothing.

Young girls study their idols and strive to emulate them. They peruse many style magazines, seeking the latest glamour techniques and trends, wanting to know what is on this season's top ten "must-have" lists, begging their parents to buy the trendy brand name clothing or luxury goods. These same youth starve themselves to be thin and attractive. Young moms spend hours at exercise gyms or spas striving for that toned body to fit into last year's bikini at this summer's pool parties.

We judge ourselves harshly when we fail to measure up. We feel we have let others down when we fail to achieve someone else's expectations of us. We even feel that they judge us, which makes us even more critical of ourselves. And I am just as guilty as everyone else. It is an unending vicious cycle.

The rat race has become so intense that we as adults are passing the same passions on to our children, driving ourselves crazy if we do not have our children in the right schools or clothed in the proper children's line. Then we continue to drive our children crazy if they do not have the same ambitions that we, as parents, have for them.

We are all guilty, like three blind mice. "See how we run? See how we run?" We run in every direction except the right one, losing our identity in the process. But what is the right direction? We have all asked ourselves this question from time to time.

In my opinion, the right direction is to seek the will of God for our lives. He knows best our gifts and talents, and he knows what is best for us; after all, he is the one who created us. Unfortunately for me due to the conflict in my spirit, my personal desire for the bright lights, the fame, and the accolades, I did not learn this until much later. Meanwhile, I continued to wander in my confusion like one of the blind mice on a running wheel.

I had read once that "not wanting something is as good as possessing it." Could I convince myself that I did not want this kind of fairy-tale life? Would "not wanting it" allow me to settle back into normal life, or would I always have a yearning for it?

There was still one string attached holding me to the fairy tale. My contract required that I enter one more international pageant, the Queen of the Pacific Pageant in Melbourne, Australia, in March 1972. The idea of being able to travel again, to be on the stage once more gave me a bit of consolation, helping me realize I could wean myself off this fairy-tale addiction a little at a time.

The Brunos wisely kept me scheduled on the road, right up until June 30, when I arrived back in Niagara Falls to crown the new Miss Dominion of Canada on Dominion Day. Meeting all the girls, sensing their excitement and anticipation, was a bittersweet time for me. I remembered my own anticipation and the "voice" and the "vision" that carried me through, and I wondered if any of these new girls might be carrying her own vision. Was God carrying her along to a new destiny as he had done for me?

I encouraged them in every aspect of the pageant, telling them what a great year I had, how meaningful it had been for me, and ensuring them of the promise of opportunity. This was all true from a material and physical point of view. I had grown and had learned a lot during this time. However, I could not share with them my sense of loss or the conflict within my spirit.

The moment arrived when I would go out on stage and present my final remarks sharing with the audience the highlights of my year. The young girl who walked across the stage that night was more confident, more sophisticated, and wiser than the young girl who had walked it a year ago. Yes, indeed, the awkward, unsophisticated, simple-minded farm girl had disappeared. In her place was the conformed protégé of Mrs. Bruno, the modeling world, the stage, and the beauty pageant circuitry. The transformation was evident and real.

I thanked everyone who had helped me during this year, but I gave all my gratitude to God who was a constant companion, keeping me grounded amidst the uproar in my spirit, so I might choose wisely the direction for the rest of my life.

Quoting from an anonymous author, I read how "I asked God for strength and health so I might be able to achieve great ambitions. Instead, he made me weak in spirit so I could learn to obey him and thus help others." This, I believe, was the reason I felt compassion for the elderly and the sick—something real that would give meaning to my life.

Continuing, I said, "I asked God for fulfillment and power so I could be happy and enjoy the praise of other people. But instead I was given humility, so that I might really feel the need of him and therefore attain wisdom." This, I believe, was the humility I felt the day I realized I was not anyone special, just a marketing tool to benefit others. When I humbly faced this truth, I desperately felt the need for God to give me his wisdom.

"I asked God for all things so I could enjoy life, instead he gave me life so that I could enjoy all things. I got nothing I asked for but everything I hoped for."

"Everything I had hoped for" were the heart victories I found with Mother and the peace I found with Father. These victories—victories that no one else knew about—were more meaningful to me than anything else that had taken place throughout the year. They were victories that gave a remarkable, powerful, and magnanimous meaning to my relationship with my parents. "Almost despite myself, my unspoken prayers were answered. I am most richly blessed!"

As I finished my comments, I commended the same spoken prayers to each of the contestants on stage that evening, telling them, "Girls, it is not whether you win or lose here tonight but whether you can walk away and say, 'I gained a lot.' It is when you are mature and wise inside, nothing else matters—not your hair, your face, or your figure. It is this internal beauty, this inner wisdom that will carry you through life making you what you so much want to be, somebody special and therefore somebody's queen." Making the final walk and taking the final bow as Miss Dominion of Canada 1970, I finally and fully understood what Mother meant when she consistently repeated to me and my sisters, "Beauty is as beauty does."

Receiving a warm applause as I stood on stage with grace, dignity, power, and conviction of thought, my only hope was to be able to live up to my own words. Can I really live up to my own words? Can I find spiritual conviction within them? Later, I would receive a letter from the mayor of Niagara Falls telling me it was the best speech he had ever heard. His letter encouraged me to try even harder to accomplish the message and to achieve the aspirations within these very pronouncements. But I knew it was certainly going to be difficult.

*   *   *

The clock had struck midnight. The gown was temporarily placed in a plastic bag, awaiting the Queen of the Pacific pageant the following March, replaced by a light blue starched nurse's uniform. The crown was replaced with a triangle-shaped nurse's cap. The Miss Dominion of Canada sash was replaced by a name tag, which did have my name on it, along with the title student nurse.

The nude stockings and high-heeled shoes were replaced by white hose and soft-soled white shoes. The false eyelashes and makeup were reserved for special occasions and outings; no longer was glamour needed in my new environment.

All my trophies, gifts, and memorabilia were placed in a large navy blue trunk that would accompany me to my small, semiprivate dorm room at St. Joseph's. Here I had a single bed. Here I shared a sink with my roommate, a shower and bathroom facilities down the hall with the other students. Here there was no pampering and no armful of red roses upon my arrival. Here the motto of the sisters of St. Joseph's was, "It is an honor to serve the sick." I had made the choice. I hoped this would indeed be the safe place I needed to find my soul.

*   *   *

"What's Miss Canada doing here?"

"Wait till she has to change a bedpan, then we'll see how pretty she really is!"

"Miss Canada, you're wanted on the hall phone. It's your manager wanting you to go on an appearance!"

"It's your photographer. You're wanted on a photo shoot!" These were the taunts and the torments being dished out by some of my fellow students at the St. Joseph's School of Nursing. Supposedly mature young women were acting like elementary school girl bullies.

These girls had no idea with whom they were dealing; they had no idea just how strong, tough, and stubborn I was. In some ways, their teasing was quite familiar to the relentless teasing I received at the hands of my brothers and sisters while growing up on the farm. Little did my tormentors know that teasing was second nature to all of us in my family. We had consistently searched for ways to play pranks on one another. I was not going to let these newly found bullies shake me anymore than I did when I was younger. I could flick them off with just the twist of my head; ignoring them with my silence was deterrence enough.

In some ways, bullies remind me of the wild tomcats that hung out in our barn on the farm, allowed to live there by Father to keep the mice population under control. Whenever provoked by our brothers, the tomcats would hiss and claw, striking out at whatever was in their path. To me, this is the same with bullies. Whenever they're jealous or insecure, provoked, or threatened, they lash out, hissing and clawing their way to overpower or control. They belittle others to make themselves look more important. They gossip and slander others for the same reasons.

It's one thing for siblings to torment and tease one another—most parents will step in and correct this unfortunate behavior—it's another for bullies to work their damage on defenseless children on the school ground or other areas where the children feel guilty if they tattle or seek support from those in authority. I feel sorry for children who do not know the meaning of the Golden Rule. I feel sorry for parents who today do not take time to teach their children, "Do unto others as you would have them do unto you." Kindness, goodness, gentleness, and self-control are more honorable and noble than acting like a bully. Bullying is an issue that is growing rapidly in our culture of impunity. Consequences for bad behavior are seemingly lacking in many cases.

As for changing a bedpan, it would be nothing for me compared to cleaning the stables and pitching manure; nothing compared to digging potatoes in the fields and getting so covered in red clay it would be caked under my fingernails, coming out of my eyes, my nose, and my ears; nothing compared to hauling logs from the forest, cutting them on a seesaw, chopping wood into logs, or throwing loads of black coal into our cellar for winter fires in the furnace; nothing compared to being sprayed by a skunk!

Yes, indeed, these girls had no idea with whom they were dealing. I was prepared for the role of nursing in ways they couldn't even imagine or know. I was actually prepared for nursing better than those who lacked wisdom and compassion.

Before long they recognized my strengths, and I won their respect and their friendship. Even the skeptical nursing instructors were amazed and pleased not only with my strength, but with my excellent grades. The relentless challenge, always before me, was to prove myself worthy, to prove myself capable. This would become the pattern for the rest of my life.

*   *   *

Sharon was aware of my challenges. She sensed my struggles to fit in. Right from the beginning she accepted me as if I was one of the girls. There was discernment and a sense of compassion about her. Sharon did not put on airs, so I found her to be natural and accommodating. She was short with long straight hair that fell below her waist. She wore it loose when we were not in uniform, but whenever we were in uniform it had to be tied up, often in braids. I nicknamed her Shaggy. We spent many hours together studying, laughing, having fun, and creating a lasting relationship. What I loved about her was that we could talk about anything, but we hardly ever talked about being Miss Dominion of Canada. It was if she sensed I was ready to move on, to find the new me, whoever that might be. I will never forget this wonderful girlfriend who was there for me when I needed her.

Special girlfriends are often hard to find, and God provides them sometimes for a season and sometimes for special reasons. Shaggy was both for a season and for a reason. She filled the empty place in my heart and the loneliness in my spirit that had once been filled by my sisters and brothers.

As we travel through the journey of life, I'm sure we have all come across special girlfriends who are there for us when we need them. We should look upon this as a blessing, a loving gift from God in a time of need, to strengthen us and to hold us up.

* * *

One afternoon in February 1972, I sat quietly in my dorm room looking out the window at the blustery, cold, snowy day. The temperatures were hovering around minus ten degrees Celsius. I was trying to write a paper, but my mind kept going back to the wintry days of my youth, to the hours spent outdoors playing with my sisters and brothers. These memories made me think of myself as a little girl once again. We would build snow forts in the orchard and form two battle teams. From either side of the fort, we would pitch snowballs back and forth. Anyone hit by a snowball would be considered dead and out of the battle. The last one standing would win the battle and come home with a hero's welcome.

That's when we crawled inside our makeshift igloo dug earlier in the side of a huge snow bank. Inside we would warm ourselves, thaw out our fingers and toes, and have a pretend hero's welcome home party. Pieces of black coal would serve as our make-believe chocolate cake and twigs from the trees would serve as war medals, strategically displayed along the wall of our igloo. This one is the Volunteer Service Medal, this one the 1939–1945 Star, this one the War Medal 1939–1945, this one the Defence Medal, and finally this one is the France and Germany Star, we declared as we replicated our father's campaign medals. What fun to imagine the honor Father must have felt upon receiving these medals as an act of service to his country. Those make-believe medals were as precious to us as our father's war medals were precious to him. As he polished them with Brasso, Father would show them off, being extra careful not to damage the colorful ribbons, all the while telling stories of how he received this medal or that medal—stories that we, as children, loved to hear. Why? I think it pleased us to know that Father had once been honored in this manner. Even Mother received the Canadian Volunteer Service Medal and the War Medal. Both Mother and Father wore their medals with great pride every Remembrance Day, celebrated in Canada on November 11.

As we continued to play in our makeshift igloo, Mother would come outdoors looking for us, yelling, "Where are you kids hiding? Get in here before you catch your death of cold!" We would just sit inside the igloo giggling, daring her to come out in her slippers to find us. She would call and call for us, her voice echoing through the silent snow-laden landscape for what seemed like miles. Perhaps even our neighbors could hear her across the open fields.

Finally one of us would feel sorry for Mother, stick our head out of the makeshift igloo, and answer her, saying, "We're in here, Mother. We'll be out in a little while. Don't worry, we're all fine." Then we would hear the front door slam shut as Mother retreated back inside, shivering from the cold.

Mother's voice across the landscape was never a match for Father's. On certain days, fresh-fallen snow covered the branches of the pine trees that lined the edge of the forest around our house. The snow would be so high and fluffy we could barely see the tops of the trees. Father, making his daily trek from the barn to the house, would catch us standing on those exposed branches, hanging onto the tops of the trees and swinging back and forth, back and forth as fast as we could. Truly, it was amazing the number of creative ways we as children found to entertain ourselves on the farm when we did not have any toys. We simply made our own fun.

Now it was Father's turn to yell at us. "You children come down from there, right now. If those branches give way, you could be buried underneath the snow. Don't you ever let me catch you doing that again!"

Up there on the top of the trees, we could hear Father's voice echoing throughout the whole countryside. It would come back around and bounce off each tree in the woods until it reached our ears. Even the squirrels were affected by his voice as they scurried back into their winter nests. Needless to say, we immediately responded to Father. There was no way any of us would ignore our father's commands as we bolted down from the tops of the trees, eager to show our obedience to him. It seemed as though we had scurried down as quickly as those little squirrels had scurried into their nests.

*   *   *

The knock on the door suddenly startled me as much as my father's voice startled me while I was up in the pine tree branches. "Are you awake?" It was Shaggy, wanting to know if I would like to go to the cafeteria for lunch.

"Not right now. I'm trying to finish this paper, but I can't seem to keep my mind on my work. I'm just not getting anywhere," I confessed to her. "I'll go with you to supper tonight, okay?"

"Okay, I'll bring you a sandwich," she offered.

"Chicken salad, toasted; no onions, please," I said. "Hopefully, I can get this done by this evening." But the moment she closed the door, my mind started wandering again, this time back to February 8, 1971, approximately one year ago.

I had been invited to attend the Snow Carnival of the South in the highlands of North Carolina at Beech Mountain and Sugar Mountain. It was the first time the International Ski Racing Tour was going south, having formerly been hosted at European, Canadian, and Rocky Mountain slopes. However with the advent of snowmaking equipment, the highlands were able to make and preserve a good covering of snow on the slopes and, therefore, to host these international races with great success. There would be approximately forty professional skiers competing for the purse. My job as a visiting queen was to promote the event on WBTV in Charlotte, North Carolina—to socialize with the guests on the slopes during the day and at several evening events—and to present the trophy to the winner of the North Carolina Ski Cup.

I was not expected, however, to lose my heart.

Bill B. was twenty-five years old, a captain in the United States Army Special Forces known as the Green Berets, having served in Vietnam as a paratrooper. He was handsome, debonair, and flirtatious; and he was assigned to be my escort at all the events. We enjoyed each other's company throughout the week. By the time I was to leave the area, we shared a mutual attraction and a couple of stolen kisses—one especially memorable. He put his hands on my face, looked into my eyes, and said, "You are bad for me!" What he meant was that he liked what he was feeling, yet he was not ready to face these new feelings. Having recently been discharged from service, he needed time to discover himself. I could understand where he was, because I was actually in the same place. We agreed to stay in touch.

We kept a long distance relationship meeting up a couple of times at other events I attended in the south, talking on the phone, and writing letters. One such letter I received from him was captivating. "I am sitting atop Grandfather Mountain," he stated, "thinking of you, wishing you were here." He shared the news of his five-year-old nephew's illness with a rare children's cancer. He asked if I would consider visiting. I believe that's when I realized I was "in love" with Bill. Just imagining him sitting "atop" the mountain thinking of me, needing me was enough to cause me to segue from the ball gown to the bride gown, from the ballroom to "Mother Goose" land. My fairy-tale imagination started envisioning a little cottage at the end of the lane with ruffled curtains in the windows, a white picket fence, and flowers in the front yard. *I have found my Prince Charming*, I thought. We will be married and live happily ever after. And the more I rode this wave, the more it filled my heart with warmth and joy on a stormy day, evidence that, psychologically, I was still living a fairy-tale reality. The only difference was that I changed from one pathway to another newer and hopefully more fulfilling and contented pathway.

*   *   *

In my mind it seemed as if I had one foot in the little cottage at the end of the lane and one foot onstage at the Queen of the Pacific Pageant. It was March 1972. I boarded a Qantas Pacific B747 from San Francisco to Melbourne, Australia, with a stopover in Fiji Islands. This was my second trans-Pacific journey, and I was delighted to be taking a short leave from nursing school, delighted to unpack my gown and national costume and to represent my country in this last international pageant. It was truly an honor to be going off to Melbourne. How many young people ever have the opportunity to travel "down under"? I felt this was more than an honor; it was actually a privilege.

Only the countries bordering the Pacific Ocean were involved in this pageant, so there were fifteen delegates instead of the usual fifty to sixty I assumed would participate. I had an unusual sense of anticipation about this pageant because my manager, Mr. Bruno, had been in conversation with the franchise owners, Mr. and Mrs. Eric Morley, the same franchise holders of the Miss World pageant. The Morleys remembered me as a delegate at the November 1970 Miss World pageant. They remembered the bookies and the odds given for a win at the Miss World. As the Morleys and Mr. Bruno discussed the pictures and biographies of the entrants, they all agreed that I had a high probability of winning the crown at this new pageant. Mr. Bruno related this conversation to me, drawing my interest back toward the stage and the limelight, closing the circle once again.

Sitting on the long, long flight to Melbourne, I was constantly daydreaming about winning the title, about a potential future with Prince Charming, and about my nursing school activities. I didn't know what was in store for my future. Everything seemed to be riding on whether I would win the Queen of the Pacific. The daydreams actually reminded me of playing make-believe with my little sister, Phyllis. *Are these daydreams for real*, I asked myself, *or just another make-believe game like when we were younger?* But the truth was that these were real-life happenings requiring major decisions.

In Melbourne, as usual many fun activities were planned for the delegates. One activity I will never forget was water-skiing in the Pacific Ocean. While out on the skis, I realized not too many yards away was a school of sharks. I could see about four to five black fins above the water. Fear came over me like I had never felt before. Even my earlier fears of the unknown, feeling my life was being squeezed out of me by a coiling snake, were never as great as this fear. Needless to say, I immediately signed the driver to stop and pointed out the sharks. "Look!" I yelled out. "Come quickly. I am so afraid." The driver did come around quickly to hoist me into the safety of the boat, laughing at me for being so scared. I breathed a sigh of relief as we raced back toward the dock.

Another escapade was attending a performance at an outdoor amphitheater. This was my first experience of a summer's evening sitting under the stars along the water's edge listening to an outdoor onstage performance. It was truly idyllic. As I relished this new experience, I again wished I had someone special to share my adventures with me. I wished my Prince Charming were here with me, and I romanticized what it would have been like to have him sitting beside me on the lawn, under the stars.

By the time I attended this pageant in Melbourne in 1972, the dust had settled on Prince Edward Island. My fifteen minutes of fame had passed as far as everyone was concerned, and I no longer received any telegrams or well wishes from back home. The loneliness was intense.

However, we soon dove into the pageant activities, rehearsals, and local media interviews. One newspaper featured a story of me and Miss California, with the headline, "Who'll Wear This Crown?" Needless to say, this brought more attention to me as a probable winner. However, it was not to be my destiny. During the week, Miss Hawaii became ill and had to drop out. Her first runner-up flew to Melbourne to take her place at the pageant. She was a delightful, personable young girl, beautiful, with golden skin and long black shiny hair—a perfect representative of the countries that border the Pacific Ocean, and she stole the hearts of the judges.

Shannon Moore, Miss California, and Norma Joyce Hickey, Miss Dominion
of Canada 1970 at the Queen of Pacific Pageant in Melbourne, Australia

I headed back to Canada, this time knowing for certain that my career as a beauty contestant was finally at an end. It was finished. I felt like Cinderella running away from the ball, but this time the clock had already struck midnight. As I ran, the questions, "Who am I?" "Where do I belong?" and "What is my purpose in life?" were more poignant than ever. The loss of another dream made my heartache for a sense of belonging deeper than it had ever been before I went to Australia. I wanted to feel a connection somewhere, somehow. Upon landing in Toronto, instead of going back to the dorm room, I booked another flight and continued on to Charlotte, North Carolina. I needed to see Prince Charming, wondering all the while, *Would he rescue me?* Obviously, my choice to enter nursing school was not filling the void in my soul nor helping me to find a safe place my heart could call home. I was still searching for that "something" to fill the deep loneliness and emptiness inside of me.

Today as I look back on my decisions, I recognize that psychologically I was making crucial life choices from a dangerously weak foundation. I was not the strong national beauty queen winner that everyone thought of me. I had learned to wear a mask with a big smile painted on it. The mask was so thick that no one could see through it, and I certainly was not about to tell anyone how I truly felt. I was scared, lonely, insecure, not bent on going back home to my roots, seeking a new place to call home and seeking someone who would rescue me. It's amazing how we tend to look at someone who appears, on the outside, to "have it all." We envy that one, often wishing the same success for ourselves. We do not stop to wonder how they are dealing with life emotionally or spiritually. We all need to be sensitive to consider that there could be much more going on in a person's life than what appears on the outside. Knowing ourselves and having a solid foundation is critical to a strong, happy, and lasting relationship when choosing a life-long partner.

Yet at the time, as Bill and I shared a wonderful romantic few days together, these thoughts were very far from our minds. We both felt a deeper connection, a deeper commitment, and a deeper desire to get to know each other even more. I was able to return to nursing school with a new song in my heart and an excitement that grows out of "being in love." I believe we talked on the phone every day for the next few months. Before Bill had even proposed to me, I was definitely creating a new fairy tale in my head. This one would be just like the ones I had read about in the books. I was certain it would not disappoint me; we would be married and we would live happily ever after. I was sure of it.

"For I know the plans I have for you," declares the Lord, "plans to prosper you and not to harm you, plans to give you hope and a future."

—JEREMIAH 29:11 (NIV)

THE IDENTITY
CRISIS CONTINUES

It was a beautiful day in the Appalachian Mountains on September 2, 1972. The leaves were not yet boldly tinged with their famous fall colors, especially at the lower altitudes. However, on the higher levels of Grandfather Mountain, close to Boone, North Carolina, there might have been a hint of color if you looked closely enough. In just a couple weeks time, the trees would be generating an extravagant tapestry of red, gold, orange, and magenta—an expression of God's creative glory.

The angle of the sun at this time of year was casting beautiful shadows under magnificently aged maple and magnolia trees in Mama Chris's garden. Mama Chris, as we all called her, was Bill's mother, a gentile Southern woman of extraordinary grace and charm. On this day, she was hosting an outdoor wedding reception for her son and his new bride.

Yes, it was following my trip to Australia, the spring of that year, when my Prince Charming proposed to me. We set a date for early September. Our long-distance relationship and commitment for a lifetime were expeditious. I bundled everything into one package—all my hopes and dreams, all my wishes and desires, including my future happiness, were heaped onto this one person, my rescuer.

Bill came to Prince Edward Island to meet my family and everyone loved him; one reason was because he picked up the vacuum cleaner and started running it all around the house. Anyone who pitches in with chores in a big family is immediately placed on the "like" list. A bridal shower was held in our honor, and we received everyone's blessings. We chose his home for our wedding because Bill's father was ill and unable to make the trip to Canada. We were married at a small church in Boone,

North Carolina, where we would live. My parents and paternal grandfather were able to travel, so they came to the wedding and Father gave me away. It was not a fairy-tale show-stopping wedding, but it was lovely and sweet. I was extremely happy to be a new bride. After a one-week honeymoon on the beautiful Carolina coastal beaches, I began pouring myself into making a precious home for us, using all the homemaking skills I learned from my dear mother and following the dream of perfection I had in my head. Additionally, I poured myself into taking on his life, his identity, as my own. His family, his friends, his hopes, his dreams were to become mine now. I put my life away. I left Prince Edward Island behind. I left Canada behind. I left my one year of nursing training behind, thinking I would finish it some day, intent on living happily ever after, desiring a large family just like Mother had.

The navy blue trunk with all my trinkets and treasures was shipped to me. It contained all that represented my former life. It was damaged in shipping, so everything was purposely removed from the trunk, stored in a few cardboard boxes, and hidden away in a closet. I didn't even place a photo of myself with my sash and tiara anywhere in our new home. They remained hidden until I started writing my memoir. This act of hiding the physical remnants of my former life actually correlated psychologically with the "putting away" and the "hiding" of selected parts of my personal identity. I was deliberate and determined to make the shift from a national beauty queen to a happy young wife, wearing a new mask with a newly painted smile on it. I wanted to meet everyone's expectations as a traditional bride and to be accepted as part of my new family. For a number of years I continued to bury my experiences and mostly my talents in order to fit wholly into this new role.

Unfortunately, sometimes fitting in is like trying to put a round peg into a square hole. I was different. My experiences had truly made me different, no matter how much I denied my past. My world had expanded beyond the lives of homemakers, school-teachers, and nurses who were now my new friends. Everyone was kind to me, but I did not seem to be able to connect. I didn't talk about my experiences unless someone asked.

And then it was as if they did not understand. But then, how could they when I didn't even understand myself? As much as we all tried, it seemed as though they were keeping me at arm's length, at a safe distance, not knowing how to act around me. It was all so strange.

These experiences reminded me of a time when, during the year as Miss Dominion of Canada, I had gone home for a visit. One evening at dinnertime, I noticed Mother had brought out the good china, treating me as a special guest in our own home. She did not intend anything unkind by this gesture. I'm sure she thought she was doing something special for me, but she didn't realize that all I wanted was to be treated like everyone else—just one of the kids.

Wherever I went, wherever I was, it seemed as though people looked at me through probing eyes, without any explanation as to why. This became an unpleasant and frequent occurrence for me that, over time, I learned to live with like some sort of physical disability.

The one person I connected with in this new role as a wife

was Mama Chris. She was like my friend Shaggy—unpretentious, natural, no hidden agenda. She welcomed me as her daughter-in-law in a most loving way, teaching me many new Southern cooking skills. I loved her so much. She was like a second mother away from home. Mama Chris could make the best homemade buttermilk biscuits you ever tasted. She kept a "dough ball" in her refrigerator, and every evening she would take out a portion of dough, roll it in flour, form biscuits in her hands, and place them in a preheated oven at just the right temperature. Whenever we were blessed to eat a meal in her home, these perfectly tasting hot biscuits were a real treat with butter and honey or homemade strawberry jam and homemade applesauce. I did everything I could to learn, but there was no way I could accomplish her talent for making biscuits, even when she gave me my own "dough ball." Mama Chris just had a unique way that no one else seemed to be able to replicate, and many others did try as much as I did.

*　*　*

Mama Chris's biscuits are a perfect metaphor for how I and many other young women try to manage our lives. We take a "dough ball" that has a certain set of selected ingredients we allow into the mix, and we define it as our "self-identity." When circumstances change in our lives, requiring us to adapt, we take a pinch of this or that, we knead it and massage it in our hands until we think the product is just right. Finally, we set the temperature and bake the product in our mind until the new identity is formed to match our new circumstances. In other words, we work at redefining our personal identity and in so doing we struggle to eliminate the conflicts within our defined roles. Sometimes it works for us, and sometimes it doesn't. Sometimes it is like piling on layers that only grow cumbersome and bothersome. Other times it feels like we are digging our own grave and burying our "true self" alive, like burying or hiding parts of ourselves in a cardboard box in the closet. What is and where is our unique human individuality? And why is it that women feel the necessity to adapt all the time? Why is it that we give up our passions and talents to suit our spouses? That's the way it was when I was a young girl.

And not much has changed. Research shows that at least seventy percent of American women today are living with a personal identity crisis. I believe this change is rapidly occurring because so many opportunities have become available to women over the past twenty, thirty, or forty years that are apart from the traditional roles of nurse, teacher, secretary, homemaker, and mother. Additionally, the rapidly changing culture and direct marketing campaigns are trying to convince women that we need this or that to be successful, beautiful, thin, acceptable, healthy, and even to be happy. We all fall prey to these persuasive claims in one way or another. Let's try this, perhaps it will work this time, we think. Perhaps this is one reason why so many people are taking "selfies" on their phones. Perhaps if they visualize themselves the way others do, they might figure out who they are. Perhaps if enough people "like" them on social media, it might convince them that they are okay. It seems as though the struggle is never-ending. Somehow, we need to teach each other that we do not have to look like Cinderella in order to be "acceptable"; somehow we need to learn there are no glass slippers. Somehow, we must realize that our perfect beauty is in Christ. The Holy Book instructs us, "Let the beauty of the LORD our God be upon us" (Psalm 90:17, niv). It states, "Your beauty should not come from outward adornment... Rather, it should be that of your inner self, the unfading beauty of a gentle and quiet spirit, which is of great worth in God's sight" (1 Peter 3:3–4, niv).

As a young twenty-one-year-old bride, I had not learned this lesson. My ability to adapt to my changing circumstances was becoming so effective I felt like a chameleon, able to evolve on the outside at the drop of a hat. However, the void in my spirit was growing so large nothing seemed to fill it—not even my new Prince Charming. Suffice it to say that he was struggling with his own identity issues, but these are his stories to tell, not mine. Neither one of us were making the other one happy for longer and longer periods of time. I began searching for ways to fill the void apart from God, running after material things and striving for pleasure. Perhaps if I clicked "my heels together three times" again, I could miraculously fill the void.

Surely, education is the answer, I thought. If I get a university degree, then others will accept me as more than a pretty face. I'll show them that I also have a brain. Perhaps I can find a career that has more distinction than a nursing career. Again I was being driven by pride and a fear of what others thought of me, desiring their approval above my own desires, not looking at my own God-given gifts and talents. So I delved into liberal arts studies at Appalachian State University while holding a full-time job, trying to satiate an insatiable appetite for defining myself and answering the question, "Who am I?"

* * *

It's amazing how a young couple can be so close together and yet so far apart. Bill and I had this uncanny ability to love each other one moment and be totally at odds the next moment. Remember, we did not fully know each other or ourselves when we married. We were dreamily "in love" with our hearts and did not bring our minds into the equation to fully know and understand each other's characteristics. Over time we discovered that we were both selfish and self-centered.

I learned once that conflict in a marriage, or any relationship for that matter, comes when one or the other partner wants his or her own way all the time—that was true for us as our tempers flared constantly. Furthermore, we never established any short-term or long-term goals as a couple. We just tried to manage and address issues as they appeared, like throwing water on a fire, one day at a time, without any direction or mature wisdom. Our foundation was not built on a solid, in-depth, and trusting relationship that is required for a successful marriage.

At the university, I learned there are three kinds of love defined in Greek terms: eros, philos, and agape. Eros is "erotic love" that comes from a couple's physical attraction to each other, thinking he or she looks great, and we want to be with that one to satisfy our physical desires. It is a self-centered love because at its center is the satisfaction of one's own pleasure. There is a strong pull for erotic love because of the desire to please or satisfy oneself, thinking our fulfillment will come in meeting this desire. Erotic love makes me "happy." Erotic love only sees the best qualities in a relationship, and it neither sees nor learns to accept another's bad qualities or faults.

Philos love, on the other hand, can be likened to the type of love that develops between friends and family members. It is accepting love, it is a give-and-take love, and it desires the best for the other person rather than one's self. Philos love is admirable and can survive the test of hardships. Relationships that begin as friendships usually are more lasting because the people involved learn about and accept each other's good and bad qualities before they become attracted to each other; the attraction often develops out of a deep-seated respect for each other's abilities.

Agape love is unconditional love that is also sacrificial love. One partner makes a choice to give to another partner even if they get nothing in return. Agape love is God-centered, based on the sacrificial love of Christ when he gave his life for us. A woman can feel this type of love when she first holds her newborn baby in her arms. It is the highest form of love, above eros and philos. It is a type of spiritual love. I believe God desires each of his children to learn this type of love. His son's life on this earth is a perfect example of how we ought to live and love. We can go through many trials and tribulations as a couple, each partner making deliberate self-sacrifices in order to learn agape love. However, in the end, it is the most beautiful "love experience" on earth. When a couple reach this level of love, it is usually unending love. Couples who live together for a lifetime will invariably say they have shared agape love.

*   *   *

I can honestly say that Bill and I shared eros love. Within three years of marriage, our eros love gave us a beautiful baby girl. She was a gift from heaven, a blessing beyond blessings. As a new mother, I understood God's unconditional agape love for the first time in my life. It was pure and unblemished. I felt I could do anything for this child, including giving up my life if it ever became necessary. If you are a mother, I am sure you know what I mean. There is nothing like bearing your own child. Many fathers feel the same agape connection to their child, and

I was certain that Bill felt it for his little daughter. We were very proud, loving parents.

We called her Miki after a chaperone I met in the Miss Universe pageant. I loved her name and remembered telling this chaperone that if I ever have a little girl, I would name her Miki. Her middle name is Lucille, after Mama Chris's sister, who never had any children of her own. We felt honored to give aunt Lucy's name to our baby girl.

I was so possessive with my little baby during the first few years, not wanting anyone to pick her up or hold her. Whenever they tried to hold her, I would give them a moment or two and then take her back. She was everything to me. For the first time in my life, the loneliness, the emptiness, and the heartache for home were gone. I had everything I needed and wanted—a meaningful purpose. As a mother, I was convinced I would protect her from all the heartache and trauma I had experienced as a child and teenager. The void was filled. I believe our daughter also filled a particular emptiness in Bill.

However, I have come to know and understand that it is not

God's will for us to fill the void in our heart with another human being, no matter how old they are or whatever the relationship might be. This can be a mistake for all the people involved. The one filling the void can feel possessed and resentful and ultimately desire to pull away from the relationship. Our innate sense of freedom dictates a definite perception of individuality and independence. It is not God's intention for another human being to meet all the spirit's demands for happiness, contentment, and joy. I believe our daughter might have sensed our possessiveness because she developed a strong, independent will early in life.

Yet in spite of our common interests in the well-being of our child, Bill and I were not able to see eye to eye. Due to difficult circumstances in our marriage and the ensuing battles over the next several years, our love never evolved from eros into philos. It is sad to say that we spent thirteen years together, but we never became friends.

I was naïve in thinking that eros love was sufficient to weather any storm. I had romanticized love, believing our mutual attraction would cause us to live happily ever after. Because of my false sense of what a perfect marriage is like, we never learned the meaning of pulling together and supporting one another. Never reaching the philos stage, we drifted far apart.

* * *

Several years passed. We moved our family from Boone to Asheville, North Carolina, in order for Bill to grow his career. Each time we made a change we would be temporarily happy, thinking a change would make us complete. Yet my unhappiness, my desire for something more returned. I was sitting at my desk one day when this overwhelming sadness came over me, combined with a strong sense of confusion. It has been my experience that when we do not stand on God's divine principles and absolute truths, confusion reigns and our path becomes torturous. My heart and mind were so mixed up I didn't know which way to turn. I got up and walked out the back door of my office, headed toward my car when I felt God calling me again. "Come and visit with me," the voice said. There was a church located next to the parking lot, and I obeyed the voice and went inside.

I sat in the sanctuary praying to God when a pastor came in. He asked my reasons for being there and whether we could pray together. I told him about my unhappiness, my confusion, and my ambition to achieve a higher education, perhaps even law school. I had already applied and had been accepted at Wake Forest University where they had both undergraduate and graduate schools, including law school. I needed two more years to gain an undergraduate degree. But how was I going to be able to move to Winston-Salem, North Carolina, when Bill and I were both employed and living in Asheville? As we prayed, I distinctly remember the pastor telling me that God wants his children to have the "desires of our heart."

"How can you be so sure?" I asked.

The pastor's response, "Because he says so in his Word."

I had never heard this before, yet for some reason I clung to these words in order to ease my sadness and the longing in my heart. The words also gave me hope that perhaps I could go back to school to achieve my dreams.

Amazingly, that very afternoon Bill called to tell me that he had been offered a transfer from his position in Asheville to one in Winston-Salem and would I like to move.

"Would I?" I declared. "Absolutely!" This was the open door I needed to be able to go to Wake Forest University and possibly law school. It was a surprising and immediate answer to prayer. I shook my head in disbelief that the prayer the pastor and I offered to God would be answered so quickly. It was certainly a wow moment; however, I did not question God's sovereignty and his willingness to insert his power into this matter. Still many hurdles had to be overcome. We needed to sell our house, and we needed enough money to be able to pay the necessary tuition and books.

I tell you this story because I want you to see how God works in our lives when we least expect it. I can honestly say I do not believe in a "name it and claim it" theology like God is some great big Santa Claus or magical genie in the sky. No, I found the pastor's statement to be true. God will give us the desires of our hearts when they line up with his will, his purposes, and his plans, when he has an opportunity to display his mighty power at work, causing a miracle to occur in an otherwise impossible situation, and when the recipients of his miracles are willing to give him all the glory for those miracles. We could never have accomplished what followed without God's hand at work.

Without any hesitation, at a time when the real estate market was in a huge slump and home mortgage interest rates were at eighteen and nineteen percent, God arranged all the details for the move to Winston-Salem. Our home was sold within a few months, allowing us to make a capital gain of twenty-five thousand dollars, enough to pay for my education and cover a portion of my lost income. Additionally, God helped us find a nice affordable townhouse near campus and a great elementary school for Miki, who was now entering the first grade.

It was not easy for me to attend school on a full-time basis, raise a young child, and maintain a home. I was taking both my major in philosophy and my minor in political science within a two-year period, in order to complete the undergraduate requirements to attend law school. The homework, the research, and the papers required for this major and minor were extremely heavy. I would stay up into the wee hours of the morning studying and writing research papers, attending classes while Miki was in school, and managing to nap every once in a while. I kept pushing myself knowing the light was at the end of the tunnel when the semester ended, all the while thinking about Mother's years of hard work raising ten children and standing on a product line in a potato factory all night long. Her words, "Hard work never hurt anyone," kept popping into my head, reminding me to keep on striving. After five semesters I completed my course work, graduating cum laude.

I did not get the opportunity to go to law school because Bill was offered another opportunity and a promotion to transfer to Charlotte, North Carolina. This was his "dream job" offer. He was being promoted to manager of the Charlotte office of his company. There were no law schools in Charlotte at the time. Again, I chose to give up my dreams for his. God had led us to

Wake Forest initially I was sure of it, but I did not follow God's leading to further my education at law school. I questioned whether it was really his plan for me after all. I subconsciously knew my heart was not pure when I chose that level of higher education. I chose it because I wanted to impress people. I chose it because I wanted to find an avenue of escape from my marriage, a way to support myself and my daughter. I have since learned that God does not honor our plans or make them successful when they are impure or outside of his will. I felt like I had actually given up on achieving my dreams, and in turn I was not following or seeking God's will any longer.

We had discussed and even threatened separation several times. Yet I will never forget this day. It was a Saturday morning. I was taking Miki to a gymnastics meet. The night before, she and I were watching a television program in which the couple divorced. During the program, she looked at me and pleaded, "Mommy, promise me that you and Daddy will never divorce."

I did not know what to say to her. However, the next morning as we were getting into the car, I relayed the conversation to Bill. I asked him if we could consider working on our marriage and seeking counseling so we could honor our daughter's request. His response: "Let's talk about this later. Now is not the right time."

Later in the week, I noticed a file folder on the kitchen counter marked "Apartment Lease." I looked inside. The lease was signed and dated on the same Saturday that we had our conversation in the driveway. Apparently, he was as unhappy as I was and more than ready to leave. Communications had totally dissolved. We were only in Charlotte a little over a year when we separated. Our daughter was ten years old.

Another big bad wolf had come along. This time his name was "divorce," and he was huffing and puffing and blowing our house down, a house that was made of straw. Bill did approach me a year or so later and tried to reconcile. We were sitting in a restaurant having dinner discussing a possible reconciliation. There was a TV playing silently in the background. Something caught my eye. I looked up and saw these words unusually displayed on the screen in large white letters, "It's time to make up!" I knew this had to be a supernatural message from the Lord. It quickened my spirit so that I looked twice to see if it was still there. I did not say anything to Bill. The message was gone, but it was etched into my mind. However, it was too late. By then my heart had grown cold and stubborn, and I ignored the decree. The circumstances, disappointments, and discouragements, combined with the huge void in my spirit, caused me to be defiant toward God. I didn't trust his leading any longer. I had already moved on and was looking forward to making other plans; independent plans, apart from God. In other words, I was going "my own way" intent on focusing on Bill's negative qualities rather than any of his good qualities. I would say Bill and I were equally responsible for the dissolution of our marriage. We succumbed to the mantra of the day, "irreconcilable differences," when we filed for divorce.

Our experience is a good lesson for everyone to learn—that in a long-term marriage relationship, it is crucial to develop a friendship, to enjoy being together no matter what, accepting and desiring the best for one another. Philos love and agape love are what make for a lasting relationship.

*   *   *

I recalled my visit to Father's grave that beautiful spring day after his passing, the same spring following my separation. It was there when I faced the fact that I was no longer close to God. He felt more like a stranger, just like Nanny Stewart felt when I stayed at her home following my accident. It was there, at Father's gravesite, when I realized I had turned my face away from God, clinging toward the wall of self-reliance, curled up in my own obstinacy. My dreams and plans were not coming true and I blamed him. *Surely it was all God's fault*, I thought. I had done everything right, didn't I? I realized my separation from God actually caused more "homesickness" as an adult than the separation from my parents at age five. It was intense loneliness. If you have ever experienced this, you will know what I am talking about. The void in the spirit is huge, like a bottomless pit.

Many people refer to this kind of emptiness as "the dark night of the soul," when you hit rock bottom in every way possible.

Furthermore, my defiance and my husband's defiance had caused us to break our little daughter's heart. This realization caused even greater sorrow, as I had never wanted to hurt her in any way. My sorrow and my regret forced me to call out to God more than ever. That's when I laid my baby's heart on his altar of mercy, asking for a special miracle in our lives.

We as parents really need to stop, to think long and hard about the decision to divorce and how it affects our children. The damage is greater than we realize. The old adage that children easily adapt is true, but another one is equally true—children are particularly sensitive to feelings of rejection. I was very familiar with these feelings because of my own youth. But now as a single parent, I had to figure out a way to erase her anger, her sense of rejection and her sense of loss. I wanted to rebuild our relationship. I wanted to feel her acceptance, her forgiveness, and I wanted her to feel "at home" in the new home I was trying to create for us. I needed her to feel secure. I did not want her to go through life as I had, not knowing where she belonged or where her home was. I did not wish this kind of loneliness, this kind of identity crisis on anyone, especially my daughter. I realized as her mother I was failing to protect her from the very trauma, pain, and disappointment that I had hoped she would never experience. Realizing my failure as a mother was heart-wrenching.

Several years later when Miki was planning to marry her college sweetheart, Andy, and create a home of her own, I remember us taking a long walk talking about marriage and divorce. She expressed the hope that her marriage would not end in divorce. We talked about the divorce of her father and me. I remember telling her how sorry I was for the pain she went through, pointing out that it is in our pain and sorrow that we develop and shape a stronger character. "Neither one of us would be the person we are today if we had not gone through these personal struggles." I believe she knew and understood that statement to be true. "Trials are what build character and persistence," I told her. It was unfortunate though that our divorce had to be the trial she would endure. It had been my hope that any trials she would face in life would have been a different sort and not one that I was responsible for causing. I relayed to her my newly found wisdom that with God at the head of her marriage, she and Andy will never have a need to divorce.

In spite of anything I might have done or not done as a mother, my daughter has always been her "own girl." She knew who she was and what she wanted from life even as a young child. Her ability to find her passions and talents has always guided her in a way that mine did not. She has an inner compass, a northern star, and a certain knowledge that I never possessed. I admire my daughter for all that she has been able to accomplish in life. She is as beautiful on the inside as she is on the outside and well loved by all who are fortunate to know her.

Despite my weaknesses and failures as a mother, she was able to find the place her heart calls "home" and to make a wonder-ful, loving home for her family. She and my son-in-law, Andy, have given us two wonderful grandchildren—a little girl, Lucy, and a little boy, Dylan. Miki and Andy are doing a remarkable job raising these children amid today's fast-paced culture; both

children are adapting well to the demands of a twenty-first century childhood. I praise God every day for answered prayers
on behalf of my daughter and her family. I praise God for these
two beautiful grandchildren who bring me so much joy and
often give me an opportunity to revisit fairyland, carrying my
imagination back to my little girl days. I thank him for coming
through for me despite my willful defiance and disobedience.
And I pray that each one of my children and grandchildren will
continue to find favor with God as they make their own personal
journey through life.

*   *   *

Have you ever been caught in an undertow and feel as though
you are being pulled out to sea? This happened to my sisters and
me once when we were younger. As much as I can recall, Barbie,
Darlene, Phyllis, and I were not too far into the water, probably
about chest to shoulder height, when we felt this unbelievable
pull around our feet. It was as if something or someone had hold
of us and was trying to take us away. Barbie was old enough and

smart enough to remember Father's instructions, "Do not fight the undertow by walking straight into the shore. Always walk parallel to the shoreline." I recall struggling, holding onto each other, so frightened, walking in a side-to-side stepping pattern until we reached ankle depth. Then we felt the undertow releasing us.

To physically experience an undertow, or "rip current" as it is correctly identified, is one thing you never forget. However, to experience the same "pull" emotionally can be a different thing. You know it is wrong for you, and you know it is dangerous. Yet the more you fight against it, the more you lose the battle.

That is how it was for me and my soon-to-be new husband Bill Dougherty (nicknamed "Bud" by his family). We were working together for several years, but right from the beginning we became excellent friends. I had great respect for him, his business skills, and his abilities. He was a king in the business world, a chief financial officer, and I was his administrative assistant—a classic tale. In addition, he had what I would call enormous respect for my talent and abilities. For the first time in my life, someone recognized that I had a brain. He was constantly acknowledging my business skills, complimenting me, encouraging me to achieve above and beyond. We communicated on a comparable level about many things, and I was invited to give my input on various corporate decisions. Being treated as a peer in a corporate environment was extremely flattering to me. I loved the respect I was receiving, and it all felt so good.

Because we spent so many hours together, including lunch breaks either in the conference room or at a nearby restaurant, we shared a lot of personal stories as well. Even though we had a significant age difference, we realized we had actually shared the same experiences while growing up. Since Prince Edward Island lagged behind the rest of the country, we both experienced no electricity or indoor plumbing and no TV in our homes during our early years. Additionally, his family experienced the Great Depression, so he knew what it was like to live in poverty and to be a survivor. We even shared the same work ethic, pouring ourselves into projects, always striving to do our best. He was taught by his parents to be responsible and to be a gentleman. Our common interests stimulated lots of conversation and laughter.

The age difference did not affect our mutual admiration for one another. The more time we spent working together, the closer we grew as friends. You could say we developed philos love. Philos love is not a bad thing between two members of the opposite sex, but when that attraction grows into something more, like an undertow, it becomes dangerous, especially when one or the other is married and has a family. When eros love developed, neither one of us planned nor expected it to happen. We fought against it. I was breaking all my own rules and one of God's commandments. Talk about confusion—it was agonizing. However, when Bud accepted a job in New York, he said to me upon leaving, "I'm coming back for you." The better thing for him and his family might have been for him to go on and never look back. But he didn't.

Within a year of his move, Bud separated, finalized his divorce, and we were married. Before we married, I spoke with a counselor. I was concerned about our age difference of twenty years but not afraid. My maternal grandmother and grandfather, my aunt and uncle, and even one of my sisters and her husband all shared an age difference. And so while the experience was not unusual, I wanted to make certain I was not getting into an unhealthy relationship. The counselor reassured me. I remember her advice, "You can always be in an unhealthy relationship with someone the same age as yourself if you respond to situations like a little girl rather than a grown woman." We discussed my strengths and abilities to act on my own free will. She thought I was safe as long as we maintained a mutual respect for one another's role as a couple, especially since we each had a strong personality.

Our marriage got off to a very rocky beginning. Our children did not welcome these changes. I can honestly say we made quite a royal mess of things. In addition, I did not have a sense of belonging, the safe place my heart calls "home" anymore than I had in my former marriage. My husband was exceptionally good to me, treating me with great respect in every way possible, loving me tenderly. Yet even in the best of circumstances, it is not easy to fit into another woman's shoes in a second marriage, especially when children are involved. It was going to be more difficult for me because my personal identity was still sabotaged, and my internal void was continuing to plague me with questions. Would I "click my heels together three times" again to find an escape, or would I let this undertow carry me out to sea?

At the appropriate time, I overheard someone say, either on TV or radio, "We can always run away from our problems, but we will have to take ourselves with us." This statement caused me to think more deeply about my personal identity crisis. Was I the cause of my own problems, my own lack of contentment, and my own lack of security? I kept remembering the words from the counselor I had visited: "Act like a woman, not a little girl." When we look at life through the eyes of a little girl, we respond like a child. However, when we look at life through the eyes of a woman, we see a more mature way of looking at things. We seek wisdom. Her words were more appropriate for my personal development and my personal identity than she realized.

I believe these words are extremely important for every woman to grasp.

I began putting these words into practice with every situation I faced. Before long, I was opening my soul once again to the safety of God's wisdom. In the Holy Book I learned, "If any of you lacks wisdom, you should ask God, who gives generously to all without finding fault, and it will be given to you. But when you ask, you must believe and not doubt, because the one who doubts is like a wave of the sea, blown and tossed by the wind" (James 1:5–6, niv).

Over a period of five years, with persistence and determination we were able to work things out, but not without a temporary separation. It was during the separation when we realized we needed to confess our disobedience to the Lord and ask for his forgiveness, both individually and as a couple. If this marriage had any hope at all, we needed to put God at the head. It was going to take the potter's hand to correct all the cracks in the porcelain of our marriage.

I remember the day we first knelt together as a couple seeking

God's face and asking him to help us. We both wept. We had come to the end of ourselves and hopefully the end of our independence. The possibility of losing our families and each other was more than we could handle. We were ready to face the consequences whatever they might be. Since neither of us knew what it was like to have a personal relationship with Christ, we had no idea how God could possibly help bring our families together, yet we unloaded everything into his capable hands.

Truly it is interesting how we as humans think we can make choices in life which go against God's will for us and believe we will come out on top. I would say to anyone reading this memoir that my many experiences have taught me that it is impossible. The wisest choice is to follow God's will. Later on when Bud and I were reunited, we started doing couples' small group Bible studies together. We learned from the Holy Book. "And we know that in all things God works for the good of those who love him" (Romans 8:28, niv).

I can just imagine the workload God had on our behalf. It must have kept him quite busy, since we have had our share of trials and tribulations, successes, and failures. However, throughout the years as we have continued to seek him, God has consistently worked all things together for the good of our marriage. As a couple, we have learned to love beyond philos love—each of our trials teaching us more and more about agape love, peace, and patience. To learn and actually apply agape love to everyday relationships and activities is the most amazing gift. It goes beyond words. Our entire family has come together extending God's grace, mercy, love, forgiveness, and respect toward one another. My daughter Miki and Bud's three children, Debbie, David, Kathy, and his three grandchildren, Michael, Patrick, and Ashley have all displayed these godly traits in commendable ways. We have been able to bond together as a blended family and grow in God's sacrificial and unconditional love, wanting the best for one another's happiness.

Yes, it was when I sought God's wisdom and stopped doubting that I felt the release of the undertow in my spirit, the release of confusion tossing me about like a wave at sea. When we stand on God's wisdom and truths, it empowers us in ways we can hardly believe or recognize. His wisdom and truth give us unbelievable strength to stand strong against any foe and feel secure. I can't stress this enough and highly recommend his wisdom to anyone who is in challenging situations. For me, seeking God's wisdom, learning about his will and developing my faith became a long and gentle learning process but it led me onward. It was not easy to change the many years of distrust and discouragement. However, as the "dark night of my soul" started subsiding, I was able to move slowly and surely toward the triumph of my spirit and toward a magnificent end to a lifelong struggle.

> He gives strength to the weary and increases the power of the weak…but those who hope in the Lord will renew their strength. They will soar on wings like eagles; they will run and not grow weary, they will walk and not be faint.
>
> —ISAIAH 40: 29, 31 (NIV)

THE UNFOLDING

Boarding a flight from Chicago to Toronto, I took my seat next to a nice-looking lady named Judy. I had the aisle, she the center, and her husband, John, sat next to the window. Although I was not in the mood, we quickly started a conversation. I was making an effort to be polite. Judy read my face. I was at the beginning of my faith-building healing process but still deeply troubled.

Judy, who didn't know my situation, chatted about her family, her three daughters, and their life in Kitchener, Ontario. The simplicity of her life, the love and joy she expressed caused me to wonder why she had so much peace. I was envious.

There are people who live together forever, I thought. There are people who find the "happily ever after" that I could not seem to find.

As her life's story unfolded, she described her personal relationship with Jesus, what it meant for her daily living and, she asked if I did also. "I don't think so," I said. I pressed my body and my head closer to the seat, trying to use her body as a barricade between me and her husband. I did not want him to hear what seemed like such an intimate conversation. Like Mother, I had never talked about my faith out loud, especially in front of a man; the fewer people who heard us, the better. Like Mother, I thought these sorts of conversations were so very private.

Judy told me she was a speaker and a singer for Stonecroft Ministries of Canada, an evangelical women's ministry that had started many years ago in the United States. She asked if I had heard about it. I hadn't and I was immediately on guard, wanting to avoid getting caught up in something or being solicited.

"What is an evangelical ministry"? I asked, trying to pronounce the word correctly.

She explained that it was an outreach ministry, and the

main purpose was to share the gospel of Jesus Christ with other women.

"I thought that was the church's responsibility," I commented.

"Many women do not attend church and never have the opportunity to learn about the love of Jesus," she explained. "Once they learn about him, amazing changes take place in their homes and their families, and they often end up finding a church home."

This piqued my interest. I was certain I needed some positive changes to take place in my own and my family's lives. Although I knew about God and had shared many special moments praying to him, I had no concept of having a personal relationship with Jesus. *How could this be so different?* I wondered.

At one point, she asked if I had heard the scripture expressed by Jesus in the New Testament, "I am the way and the truth and the life. No one comes to the Father except through me" (John 14:6, niv). I told her I had.

"When I was younger, those words meant a lot to me," I confessed. "But now they don't seem to hold the same meaning, and I don't understand. It actually feels like God is so far away from me."

Judy smiled, assuring me that if those words meant something to me at one time, they would mean something to me again. She was certain that God would not start something good in me that he would not finish.

What assurance, what belief! I thought. *What a strong faith!*

She told me she would pray for me and send me some reading materials. I gave her my address and phone number, again just to be polite, but I did not expect her to actually send the material nor plan to read it if she did. My focus was on resolving my personal issues, not on developing my spiritual life. But what I was about to learn is the two always go hand in hand. It was March 1994.

I received a package in the mail as Judy had promised. It was a Good News New Testament and a small Bible study booklet on the gospel of Mark. I had never studied the gospels, and I wasn't sure how to go about it. Unfortunately, I did not open either book. I had still not learned the benefits of opening the Holy

Book and reading what was inside. I was certainly not interested in sitting in a women's circle at church or anywhere else for that matter, doing a Bible study. Besides, I had always thought these women "put on airs" and made themselves out to be "holier than thou." I wasn't about to join their ranks. Attending church on Sundays was as far as I ever intended to go on this journey.

Judy kept calling me on the phone—long distance, no less, back when long distance was expensive. She asked if I was going to church or any classes. "No, not right now," I responded, "but I am thinking of joining a choir, as I love to sing." Judy encouraged me even more.

I was remembering the joy Father had when he sang in the choir with his brothers and friends. I remembered the acceptance he felt amongst his church family. Perhaps I could feel the same joy Father felt when he sang those old hymns. His favorite was "In the Garden," and he was always singing it. We often sang it together, shouting it out loud as a matter of fact. I wondered what made that hymn so special to Father. I wished I had asked him when he was alive. Perhaps it carried him through many difficult battles when he was in the war. Perhaps he shouted it out loud with his buddies as they lay together in the trenches looking up at the stars, wondering what danger might lie ahead. Or perhaps he sang it to drown out the painful moans and cries of his wounded buddies during a long night. Whatever the reason, the hymn had become a beacon of light to him, and he held onto it very tightly.

I loved the refrain, "And he walks with me and he talks with me and he tells me I am his own; and the joy we share as we tarry there, none other has ever known." I thought about those words, "He walks with me, and he talks with me" and "He tells me I am his own." Did Father know a secret about having a special friendship with God? Had Father discovered a great and mighty mystery that others, including me, failed to recognize?

I remembered God walking with me through my recovery as a teen, but I did not experience him "talking" with me to any extent. I did not experience him telling me I am his own. I remembered communing with him through nature. I remembered a peace, but I did not feel a joy like "none other has ever known." I remembered the "voice" and the "vision" of going to the Miss World and sharing the stage with Bob Hope, but I didn't have any conversational "talks" with God as the refrain suggests. To me, God was "out there, somewhere." I did not know he could be as close as a dear friend. These thoughts were intriguing.

Ever enthralled by fairy tales, I was always searching for the "happily ever after." I did not realize there was a difference between "being happy" and "being joy-filled." I was about to learn that happiness depends upon the circumstances of each day; one thing can make us happy, another thing can make us sad. But joy is something we experience regardless of our circumstances. Joy doesn't come and go like happiness. Joy stays with us, giving us contentment no matter what our situation might be.

I recalled walking in Father's footsteps when, as a child, we tread our way to the two-room schoolhouse through the winter storms. Perhaps I would follow in Father's footsteps once again by singing in the choir. Perhaps this time, my stride would match Father's big stride as he led me through the storms of my life. My hope in joining the choir was to find that joy Father experienced as he tread through his own storms—a joy like "none other has ever known."

"Lord, help me to find this joy," I prayed. "I need it so very much. Help me to find that safe place Father had found, even in his pain!"

One day I called the local United Methodist church. It was a white church with a majestic steeple, just like the one I attended as a young girl, but somewhat larger, with huge white columns at the front door. I asked if I could transfer my membership from the last church I had attended years ago and join the choir. They agreed, and before long I was attending church again, singing in the choir and making some wonderful lady friends. However, I was still resisting joining any women's circle. It was not for me!

* * *

"It's Judy!" my husband called out. We were living together again, trying to make our marriage work, trying to blend our families, trying to find a way to put God at the head of our home as Judy and her husband had done. Neither of us wanted our marriage to fail. "She wants to talk to you on the phone."

Not again, I thought. She is so persistent! When I answered the call, Judy had an unusual excitement in her voice. "We were praying for you," she said.

"Who's we?" I asked.

"Me and a bunch of other ladies!" she responded. "We want you to start a Christian Women's Club in your area!"

Oh no, I thought. "What's a Christian Women's Club?"

I was certain it was one of those women's circles from which I had always shied away. Judy explained that it was an event that is held at a country club or a restaurant. Women get together for fashion shows and other interesting topics, have lunch or dinner, get to know one another, and hear a special speaker share her personal testimony. "This is something you will love!" she exclaimed. *No, no!* I thought. But the truth is God was softening and melting my heart with the special hymns I had been singing in the choir. He was softening my heart as I took long leisurely walks every day, communing with him once again through nature as I had done when I was a young girl.

For the first time, I was open to her ideas. I liked fashion shows, and I liked planning parties. I liked the Christian friends whom I had met in the church choir. They were not the "holier than thou" ladies I thought they might be. These ladies actually realized and shared that without their faith, they were totally and completely lost.

I had been calling myself a Christian just because I was raised that way. However, in the past, I would go to church on a Sunday, sit in the pew next to a stranger, listen to the message, and leave. That was the extent of my spiritual journey. What I could not understand then is why the messages I heard on those Sundays were not penetrating my heart. But something different happened to me on this day.

What deeply touched me from Judy's call was hearing that a group of women, strangers whom I didn't even know, had spent time praying for me! This was most unusual! I never heard about strangers praying for other strangers. I was so touched by this news I agreed to have the regional representative from Stonecroft Ministries, Inc. contact me so we could make plans to possibly start a Christian Women's Club in my area. Within a few weeks, we had set a date.

We hosted an introductory coffee at our home. Forty-eight women from our community attended. All were interested in planning outreach events at the country club. I was asked to chair the monthly events for a two-year commitment. I declined, thinking I was not qualified or worthy to head up a Christian ladies' organization, thinking of my past sins, thinking of the unforgiveness and the condemnation I held against myself. I knew my own heart, and it was not pure. Surely, God would not want me to lead this organization. I recommended another friend.

But God did not leave me alone. Through restlessness and other stirrings, he kept prodding my heart to accept the position of chair. I kept thinking I should have said yes. Many nights during that period of time, I would awaken to see 3:33 on the digital clock. When it happened a couple of times, I thought it was coincidence. When it happened a couple more times, I thought it was an odd experience. When it happened a few more times, I thought it was most unusual. But still I did not understand why. The regional representative called about a month later to let me know my friend also declined the leadership position. She asked again if I would accept. This time I told her, "Yes, if you and Stonecroft Ministries have confidence in me, then I will accept."

I received the leader's training materials in the mail. I anxiously opened them, wanting to learn how to do the very best job. It has always been my nature to pour myself into any work or project that I undertake. Written there on the first page of the leader's manual were the words used as the basis of the ministry. They were from the Holy Book: "Call unto me and I will answer you and tell you great and unsearchable things you do not know" (Jeremiah 33:3, niv).

I could not believe it! I got cold chills all over my body as I realized the connection with the digital clock 3:33 experience. This was the first time God had supernaturally spoken to me using the Holy Book. He was telling me, through this experience, that he would walk alongside me and show me great and mighty things that I did not yet know, that he would be my teacher. My job was to seek him and call out to him for his answers.

For the first time, I realized that God could speak to us using his very own words. I had heard this before in church, but I had never experienced it coming directly from him in this way. Most of the time while in church, I had just gone through the motions like rote memorization, without any thought, feeling, or connection.

To actually experience his voice through his Word was absolutely stunning. To actually experience his guidance and direction through his Word was beyond my imagination. I realized in that moment that his Word, the Holy Book, is the mind, the spirit, and the heart of God! I had discovered the most amazing treasure, and I wanted it, all of it. "And he talks with me." Wow!

*   *   *

Over the next two years, I chaired the Christian Women's Club with great success. Holding a monthly outreach meeting and listening to special speakers sharing their personal testimony of how God had changed their lives was a new journey for me and many other women. We bonded together in close friendships, we worked in unity on planning teams, we met once a month for prayer, and we followed up with new believers, women who noted on a card that they had an interest in getting to know Christ in a more personal way.

We started many small group Bible studies using the study materials that Stonecroft Ministries had produced. These studies were easy to follow and understand, each one constantly directing us to look up verses from the Holy Book and to focus on what God was teaching us through his very own words. I was actually able to remember what I was learning and to apply the teachings to my life on a daily basis. I was also finding that God has an answer in his Word to almost every situation we face in life. That was another truly amazing experience for me. As each woman's heart was being renewed, restored, and touched by new and deeper knowledge of our Savior, Jesus Christ, there was a rippling effect throughout our families and our community. It was just like Judy had shared with me on the airplane in 1994.

*   *   *

But something deeper was happening to me. God was asking me to look into his mirror of truth, to face my own sins, to look at my own heart the way he sees my heart. I cautiously took these steps. I wanted to hold on to the fact that I was not a "bad girl."

I had been a victim of my circumstances. Surely that was the truth! Letting go of the victim role and looking into this mirror was not easy. At first, I would just peek into his mirror of truth. I acknowledged a few sins but nothing big.

Then one day as I looked deeper, the reflection in the mirror said to me,

You are not the fairest one of all. You have done this and you have done that. You are a grown woman and you must take responsibility before God for your own wrongdoing. You must confess to me what you hold in your heart, so I can cleanse your

heart, forgive you, pronounce you not guilty, and help you to realize that you are "my own," my child. After all, that is why Christ died for you.

The thoughts continued, *Don't you understand that I am a God of justice? Don't you understand what justice means? Justice is one of my attributes, and it flows from my holiness, my righteousness. A holy and righteous God cannot be in relationship with someone who has been living in sin. Sin is a crime against me, and my justice demands a penalty. You can never be good enough on your own to pay the penalty to satisfy my sense of justice.*

Have you not yet learned the only way to me is through the death of my son, Jesus, who paid the penalty for you? Have you not yet learned the true meaning and purpose of the cross and the reason why Jesus died for you? Do you think all your good work is saving you? Have you not seen that I would have given my only son just for you, so that you could come to me pure, whole, and undefiled? Have you not yet learned this great mystery that I am showing you, this great and mighty thing? I love you, I forgive you, I will set you free from the bonds you have

tied around your heart, but you must give them over to me.

Now I could see why God seemed so far away from me over these last few years. Now I could see why the messages on Sunday mornings were not penetrating my heart. I was blocking God's presence with my sin, my unwillingness to confess, my unwillingness to take responsibility for my own actions, my unwillingness to drop the banner that boldly states, *I am a victim.* I was wearing that banner around my heart quietly, privately, and sometimes pridefully—just as proud as when I wore the Miss Dominion of Canada banner. I had to let it go, admit my sins, ask God for forgiveness, and acknowledge the reason why Christ died on the cross for me. This was the only true way to the Heavenly Father. I vividly recalled my teenage experience at the altar when the minister said, "This bread represents my body broken for you. This wine represents my blood that was shed for the forgiveness of your sin." I understood now that God was showing me the way to himself back then, out of his great love and mercy for a broken young girl. He knew I was too young to understand anything more at that time.

Now, though, he was teaching me another "great and mighty" truth, showing me the way to himself through his justice and the true purpose of the cross. He was continuing his work in me as he promises, "For any good work I begin in you, I will see it through to completion" (Philippians 1:6, niv).

I sat there in the quietness of my bedroom, stunned by the thoughts. It was a beautiful day outdoors, and the water was sparkling like diamonds on the lake where we lived. The sunlight was pouring into the small sitting room, creating shadows that were dancing on the wall. As I read the words in my open Bible, I knew it had to start in this moment. I knew it had to start with me. "Create in me a pure heart, O God, and renew a steadfast spirit within me. Do not cast me from your presence or take your Holy Spirit from me. Restore to me the joy of your salvation and grant me a willing spirit to sustain me" (Psalm 51:10–12, niv).

"Dear God, grant me a willing spirit as your word says. Create in me a pure heart." I knew what God was asking "me" to do. No one else could do this for me. Many grievances ran through my mind like a slow motion movie. I witnessed the wrongdoing I had done, the lies I had told, and the hurtful words I had said about another. The images were so painful to me. *They must be even more painful to God,* I thought as tears of regret ran down my cheeks.

I confessed that I was not the fairest one of all. I confessed that I was indeed a sinner, no longer able to hide under the guise of being a victim. "Oh God, forgive me." I read aloud these verses over and over again, asking God to stay with me as he had throughout the years, during those times when I had allowed him. I asked him to remain present, to keep his Holy Spirit with me, to restore the joy of my salvation, and most importantly to let me understand the deeper meaning of Christ living in my heart as my Lord and Savior. "What does it really mean? What does it look like?" I truly wanted to know, and so I started on a new journey to find out what it means to have a personal relationship with Christ, to have him living within my heart, to know the "joy like none other has ever known."

You will seek me and find me when you seek me with all your heart.

—JEREMIAH 29:13 (NIV)

THE HEART OF THE MATTER

A journey seeking a personal relationship with Jesus Christ can be exciting, adventurous, and very challenging. Having spent so many years believing in a fairy-tale reality, I was determined to make certain this journey was real. I needed to be truly confident the Holy Book was not another "once upon a time" storybook.

Jesus said, "I am the way and the truth, and the life" (John 14:6, niv). The truth? What could this possibly mean? Could we find the truth in one person's life, purpose, and sacrifice? I had been searching for the truth for such a long time. All I seemed to find in this world in many cases was deceit, duplicity, deception, and pretensions—everyone for himself or herself. I also speak of my own behavior, so I am not speaking against anyone.

Even some of the women in the Christian Women's Club we had formed were seeking the truth; they did not have the answers either. I guess you could say we were the "seekers" in the group. But on the other hand, there were women who had this unbelievable peace and joy even when their lives were going through terrible circumstances: illnesses, death of a spouse or child, financial worries, and so on. These women were intriguing because they had what I needed—a joy like "none other has ever known."

Years earlier, when I was blessed to be able to go to Wake Forest University, I studied many of the greatest philosophers and political scientists. Yet I certainly did not find any truth in those studies. There were a lot of opinions on whether God existed, on right and wrong moral actions, on whether we actually have free will, on what reality is or is not, and many other such questions. But there were no definitive answers. The one thing my study of philosophy and political science gave me was a tenacious ability to rationalize and think more critically and to understand someone else's argument if different from mine.

That is exactly where I found myself when it came to undertaking this challenging new journey. I decided to approach it from a factual and historical perspective while at the same time planning to let God be my teacher as he had promised to do, to show me "great and mighty things." How could I go wrong with that approach?

Unlike some of the renowned philosophers I studied, I did believe in the existence of God. That was never a question for me. My personal experiences throughout life had confirmed this realization and knowledge. But I did not want this knowledge to be based solely on subjective reasoning or subjective feelings. I needed to know that God had a purpose and a plan in making himself known to me and to mankind. And this business about having a personal relationship with his son—could he possibly live within my heart as so many followers of Jesus Christ claim as truth? And would this truth set me free from my constant soul-searching, lack of contentment, and a desire to always escape my circumstances? Could I find the place my heart calls "home" within this truth?

I chose to start with the history of Jesus' life. Having once studied philosophy of law, a title caught my eye at the Christian bookstore, *Evidence That Demands A Verdict, Volume 1*, written by Josh McDowell. The subtitle was "Historical Evidences for the Christian Faith." The back cover stated that McDowell's works were "an unparalleled defense of Christianity."

It further stated, "There are answers—scholarly, intelligent, well-grounded answers. Answers backed by solid, historical evidence."

The back cover further listed a group of questions and promised to provide the answers to those questions in this book:

- Is the Christian faith built upon good solid evidence?
- Can the Bible withstand the onslaught of the most scholarly skeptics?
- Is the Bible a reliable historical record?
- Was the resurrection a hoax or one of the greatest historical events?

- Were the events surrounding the life of Jesus Christ accurately foretold centuries before his birth?

- Why was Jesus Christ profoundly different from any other man who ever lived?

As I perused the table of contents, I knew this was the book I needed to study. There were topics such as "The Bible: I Trust It," "How Was the Bible Prepared?" "Jesus, a Man of History," "The Resurrection: Hoax or History?" "God at Work in History and Human Lives," and not least of all was a section entitled, "He Changed My Life"—The testimony of how a relationship with Jesus Christ transformed the author's life. All of these topics piqued my interest, and I felt they would help answer my intellectual questions objectively. My goal was to give me the working confidence I needed to believe the Holy Book as real, not another happily-ever-after fairy tale, Santa Claus, Tooth Fairy, or Easter Bunny tale.

As usual, I dug fervently into this new study. One of the first things I was able to confirm, both through *Evidence That Demands a Verdict* and through the Holy Book, was that God has not only given us a mind; he wants us to use our mind to think, to question, to examine our own doubts, and to discern his truths. No question is too difficult for God as he clearly states, "For my thoughts are not your thoughts, neither are my ways your ways," declares the Lord. "As the heavens are higher than the earth, so are my ways higher than your ways and my thoughts than your thoughts" (Isaiah 55: 8–9, niv). As I read these verses from the Holy Book, I thanked God that he was not offended by me asking him relevant questions, encouraging me even more with instructions in 1 Peter 3:15 (niv), "Always be prepared to give an answer to everyone who asks you to give the reason for the hope that you have. But do this with gentleness and respect, keeping a clear conscience...." I realized my studies would give me the preparation I needed to answer even my own deeply spiritual questions.

Therefore, as I share my journey with you, the reader, I specifically state that what I share is without boldness and arrogance, but with gentleness and respect. I am definitely not a biblical scholar. I only share what I have learned from my own experiences while seeking to develop a personal relationship with Jesus Christ and to find a joy like "none other has ever known."

At the same time, though, I encourage anyone who is interested in developing his or her own faith to take a similar personal and objective approach. There are many historical books out there for our education. God does not want us to walk alongside his son with a blind faith. This is clear in the gospels of Matthew and Mark. For instance, a lawyer who was seeking intellectual answers, just like I was, asked Jesus, "Teacher, which is the Greatest Commandment in the Law?" (Matthew 22:36, niv). Jesus answered him by saying, "The most important one is this:… 'Love the Lord your God with all your heart and with all your soul and with all your mind and with all your strength'" (Mark 12:29–30, niv). Hence, Jesus was saying that to be knowledgeable of Jesus "with our mind" is every bit as important as being knowledgeable of him "with our heart and soul and strength."

To know the historical Jesus as one who was truly born, one who lived and died on this earth, gives us confidence in the

Holy Book as real. *Evidence That Demands a Verdict, Volume I* confirms the historicity of Jesus, his birth, life, death, and, most importantly, his resurrection. It does so by deliberately and carefully going back into antiquity to confirm the reliability of manuscript evidence; to study and outline the written resources of the great historians like Irenaeus, Ignatius, Flavius Josephus and others; to review and factually dispute the many skeptics; and to corroborate the stories of the gospel writers who personally claimed to be eyewitnesses to the life, the miracles, the death, and the resurrection of Jesus Christ—eyewitnesses who confirmed their claims among numerous audiences who could have easily disputed those claims. An example of this is seen in Acts when Peter addressed the crowd, saying, "Men of Israel, listen to this: Jesus of Nazareth was a man accredited by God to you by miracles, wonders and signs, which God did among you through him, as you yourselves know" Acts 2:22 (niv). And further, "God has raised this Jesus to life, and we are all witnesses of the fact" Acts 2:32 (niv). Yes, it wasn't just the gospel writers who were eyewitnesses, but also a great number of people. Furthermore, these very same gospel writers were willing to martyr their own lives for the sake of future believers and for the growth of God's kingdom.

So I asked myself this question, *Would I martyr my life if I believed the resurrection to be a tale, a false tale?* Would you? For me, the answer is, "No, absolutely not!" And I'm sure it is for you also.

This conclusion led me toward another intellectual and objective inquiry. Can we trust the Holy Book as the inerrant Word of God as so many people claim? I took a logical approach to find an answer to this question. In the study of the philosophy of logic at the university, I learned the logical sequence called syllogism. To be logical, two premises are tested against one another; for example, premise two is tested against premise one. If both of the premises are valid arguments, then we can draw a strong conclusion. The historical Jesus who lived, died, and was resurrected stated, "Heaven and earth will pass away, but my words will never pass away" (Matthew 23:35, niv). Also, Jesus says this while praying to his Heavenly Father "Your Word is truth" (John 17:17, niv). And the Old Testament prophet Isaiah stated, "The grass withers and the flowers fade, but the word of God endures forever." Finally we learn, "It is impossible for God to lie" (Hebrews 6:18, niv). Confirming these statements in the New Testament, the apostle Paul wrote, "All Scripture is God-breathed and is useful for teaching, rebuking, correcting and training in righteousness..." (2 Timothy 3:16, niv).

Therefore, looking at all these statements we can put together a logical argument. Premise one: the Bible is the God-breathed, God-inspired Word of God; Premise two: God cannot lie. Conclusion: Therefore, the Bible is the inerrant Word of God.

This approach to finding a personal relationship with Jesus was teaching me a lot of things. I learned that there are well over one thousand accurately fulfilled prophecies proclaimed in the Old Testament—prophecies that, when studied, give even more credibility and reliability to the Holy Book as the inerrant word of God. These prophecies span several centuries. If you study them, you would find, as I did, there is no way they could have been purposely enacted or staged by man.

However, all this knowledge was not leading me into a personal and intimate friendship with Jesus Christ as I had hoped. Yes, my research was giving me an "intellectual" faith. It was giving me a basis on which to trust the Word and the promises of God. I was learning all "about" God. But where was this relationship that others claimed to have received? I was still missing something.

And then it happened! One day, I was reading a story in the Gospel of Mark.

That day when evening came, he said to his disciples, 'Let us go over to the other side.' Leaving the crowd behind, they took him along, just as he was, in the boat. There were other boats with him. A furious squall came up, and the waves broke over the boat, so that it was nearly swamped. Jesus was in the stern, sleeping on a cushion. The disciples woke him and said to him, 'Teacher, don't you care if we drown?' He got up, rebuked the wind and said to the waves, 'Quiet! Be still!' Then the wind died down and it was completely calm. He said to his disciples, 'Why are you so afraid? Do you still have no faith?'

—MARK 4:35–40, NIV

That question Jesus asked of his disciples he could have easily asked of me. "Do you still have no faith?" As a matter of fact, I thought he was indeed asking me that question! After all God had done for me, I realized I had not put my faith and trust in Jesus, the person. Yes, I had "experiential faith," experiencing the presence of God at various times in my life. Yes, I had now discovered this "intellectual faith" through my studies. But I still had not yet developed a "triumphant faith" whereby I could yield and surrender the control of my life to Jesus as Lord of my life.

Oh my, I still have much to learn. How do I do this?

I thought again about the great commandment, "Love the Lord your God with all your heart and with all your soul and with all your mind and with all your strength" (Mark 12: 29–30, niv). I raised the questions: How can a loving God command love? Did he not give us free will? Don't I have a choice in this? Don't I get to act on my own free will?

These questions stimulated deeper thinking. From what I had learned and experienced about God throughout my life, he had never forced me to love him. He never forced me to believe in him. During the times when I did walk closely with him, I had always felt him "knocking on the door" as the Holy Book says, "Here I am! I stand at the door and knock. If anyone hears my voice and opens the door, I will come in and eat with that person, and they with me" (Revelation 3:20, niv).

I felt I had loved him and believed in him "on my own" out of a deep sense of gratitude for his love, his mercy, his grace, his forgiveness, and his peace toward me at a time when I needed these things. He had made this so easy for me. I had heard him knocking, and I had opened the door. But mine was really a one-sided relationship. I received all the benefits of his love, but I did not have fellowship with him. Think about this for a moment. If a guest knocks on the door and you invite him in to eat with you, you sit and have fellowship with one another. You talk and get to know each other in a personal way. You decide whether you like his company and, if so, you spend more and more time with each other in relationship. It is a give and take. I was beginning to see that I had taken from God all these years, but I was not giving anything back to him. My love and my gratitude were felt by me but never truly expressed back to him.

Jesus said, "Love the Lord your God with all your heart and with all your soul and with all your mind and with all your strength." In other words, there is no halfway in loving God. In a relationship with him, he wants our all. Why does an omniscient, omnipotent, omnipresent God want me to love him with all my heart, mind, and strength? Perhaps one reason he wants our all is because he has great plans for us, as he proclaims in the Holy Book, "For I know the plans I have for you, declares the Lord, 'plans to prosper you and not to harm you, plans to give you hope and a future'" (Jeremiah 29:11, niv). Additionally, his Word tells us, "To those who believed in his name, he gave the right to become children of God" (John 1:12, niv). And further, John makes this statement, "For God so loved the world that he gave his one and only Son, that whoever believes in him shall not perish but have eternal life" (John 3:16, niv). So here is this almighty, sovereign God offering me valuable gifts—plans to prosper me, plans to give me hope and a future, the right to become his child, and everlasting, eternal life—all of this if I believe, all of this if I have the faith that Jesus was asking me to have, the faith to trust that he has done and will do all that he promises to do.

I had to ask myself another question: Are these gifts valuable to me, enough to cause me to love him with all that is in me, enough to surrender my life to Jesus as Lord and Savior, enough to relinquish the control of my own will to Jesus? These were indeed questions I needed to answer on my journey to find a personal relationship with Jesus.

* * *

Just like two sisters, I thought. *Just like me and my sisters.* We were always quarreling over who would do this chore or that chore and whose turn it was to work while the other one rested. The quarreling was relentless, especially when we were teenagers and each of us wanted our own way. And quarreling is just what was taking place when Jesus went to visit the biblical Mary and Martha.

According to Luke 10: 38–42 (niv), Jesus had arrived at their home, knocked on the door, and they invited him in. Martha busied herself making preparations for a meal while Mary sat and visited with Jesus. Martha grew increasingly resentful and angry toward her sister for not helping in the kitchen. Eventually, she complained to Jesus. "Martha, Martha," the Lord answered, "you are worried and upset about many things, but few things are needed—or indeed only one. Mary has chosen what is better, and it will not be taken away from her" (Luke 10: 41–42, niv).

I could see a lesson in this story. Jesus knocked on the door. Both Martha and Mary invited him into their home. However, it was Mary who opened the door of her heart. It was Mary who sat with Jesus, listened to him, had fellowship with him, and was building a relationship with Jesus. This was a lesson I needed to learn. My two-year commitment as chair of the Christian Women's Club had come to an end. I was asked by the ministry to take another "busy" position as an area representative. But I declined, choosing instead to sit at Jesus's feet, just like Mary, to listen to him, to talk with him, to have fellowship with him, to worship him, to abide in him and, more importantly, to learn from him. I needed to learn how to pray other than little rote memory prayers—to learn to truly communicate with Jesus. The role as a prayer leader with Stonecroft's Christian Women's Club would not only give me the tools I needed to learn how to pray, it would teach me how to lead a prayer group. This is what I chose, "the better thing."

* * *

There was a yellow sticker purposely placed on the door next to the doorbell reflecting the words, "Come on In!" Several of the team members from Christian Women's Club were gathering at a friend's house for prayer. We usually met once a week at different homes for planning, Bible study, and prayer. The sticker had become a welcome sign to all who came; it meant that the home was open. It also meant that the hostess's heart was open to anyone, friend or stranger. I loved this warm approach we developed with each other. It reminded me of my mother's home in Prince Edward Island. In her later years, when all the children had left the nest, her door was always open to anyone who came along.

Mother even had a sign over the door that read, "Sit Long. Talk Long. Laugh Long." And many people did respond. Her door became a swinging door. You would never know when someone might drop in. How I wish all our neighbors and friends could be like this nowadays. Yet our pretensions and our perfections have paralyzed us to an ever-increasing degree. We hesitate to open our home, afraid we might be judged if everything is not in perfect order. Oh, how we miss out on so much friendship and laughter with one another because of our own self-imposed rules.

This day, though, as usual the hostess was in the kitchen preparing coffee and snacks for us to enjoy. I was standing around greeting everyone and listening to the conversations. Already, after two years in this role as prayer leader, I was reaching the place where I did not have to write all my prayers down on paper.

My fellowship and friendship with the living Lord were growing. I heard him whisper to me, "Be still and know that I am God!" It was spring. Easter was right around the corner, so his death and resurrection were particularly foremost in my mind. As I stood in the kitchen with a cup of coffee in my hand, amongst all the greetings and the chatter, I remember clearly and quietly talking to the Lord, saying, "I'm here. I know it's you. Jesus, you have given me so much. I wish I could give something back to you." And then I realized what I could do. Just like that, I said, "I know what I can do, Jesus! I can let you live in my heart. You gave your life for me. You died for me because of your great love. The least I can do is give you a place to live. Come, Jesus, come live in my heart!"

Suddenly, it seemed like time stood still. I was recalling the image of a young girl crawling under her bed to find an old shoebox. It was placed in the far corner surrounded by dust and a loose rug that always seemed to get kicked under the bed. The shoebox had a lid on it and was wrapped tightly with several rubber bands. Imprinted on top in bright purple crayon were the words "Do Not Touch." It was her treasure box. Hidden inside were all that reflected the creative side of her: poems, short stories, sketches, drawings, letters written but never mailed. But more importantly were her secrets and the thoughts she had jotted down because Father had told her and the other children, "Be seen and not heard." She could still hear his words echoing in her head. How then was she ever to express herself? Writing made the difference for her. Writing gave her the unique ability to go deep inside her mind, sometimes without any conscious consent, to explore the recesses and to find what needed to be revealed.

Almost immediately, as time seemed to stand still, I realized the image of the young girl crawling under the bed was actually a memory of me. I had learned to express myself through writing. The unfortunate thing is that I did not reveal these hidden treasures to anyone, not even my little sister Phyllis. I protected them with my life. Yes, I had learned to write to express myself, but I had also learned to hide my thoughts and emotions. No one was allowed to see the inner me. I was afraid I would be teased and tormented for being creative, for thinking the thoughts I thought, or believing the things I believed. In other words, I had no confidence in the inner part of me because I was actually putting my "self" on paper—a self that needed expression but also a self that needed protection.

As I stood in my friend's kitchen that day quietly communing with Jesus, I heard him whisper another message: "For where your treasure is, there your heart will be also" (Luke 12:34, niv). Jesus was helping me to recognize that which was truly hidden inside my treasure box all those years; that which was also taken out of the navy blue trunk and hidden inside cardboard boxes, placed in closets and attics. It was my heart, and it was time to open the lid and reveal all that was inside. He promised to be my protector. "But the Lord is faithful, and he will strengthen you and protect you" (2 Thessalonians 3:3, niv). I hold to his promise of protection even now as I reveal all my inner thoughts and feelings to you through the writing of this memoir.

It was settled then. After all this time, I heard his knock and finally opened the door. I surrendered my heart, my life, and my will to the living Lord. I would love him with all that was in me, as he had commanded us to do. When I started on this exciting journey to find a personal relationship with Jesus, I had made a mistake. I thought what I needed was to learn to love Jesus "with all my mind." But it was not my mind after all that needed to be opened, protected, and nurtured. It was my heart that was all tied up with rubber bands. I needed to learn to love him "with all my heart."

> Their hearts are secure, they will have no fear; in the end they will look in triumph....
>
> —PSALM 112:8 (NIV)

THE TRIUMPH

It is one thing to say I'll love Jesus with all my heart, mind, and strength, and it is certainly another thing to actually do that. Apparently, it happens all at once for some people; but for others, it takes time. For me, it would definitely be a process. I wanted to be sure; I wanted to trust. And although many things had happened thus far that should have solidified my trust, there had been several exploits in my life that certainly undermined my ability to trust.

But more than that, I was still caught up with worry and concern. What would other people think if I became what some called a "Bible Thumper" or a "Jesus Freak"? I had already come quite far down this road. How much further did I wish to go?

These were the same insecure, fearful feelings I had when I was younger, worried about what other people might think of me and my sisters because we were the janitors of our schools. I knew where this type of insecurity had come from. It had grown out of my desire as a young girl to be a "people pleaser" and a "fixer" in order to bring change into our home. It was also the same fear that, throughout life, had kept me in a constant state of confusion and change, trying to suit everyone else and not recognizing my own God-given gifts and talents. I realized that this was indeed a prideful spirit—one that needed to be quenched.

Oh, what to do? Did I really want to go further in this faith journey? Jesus himself warns, "So, because you are lukewarm—neither hot nor cold—I am about to spit you out of my mouth" (Revelation 3:16, niv). *Oh, my gosh.* I thought. I do not want Jesus to spit me out of his mouth or turn away from me because I am wishy-washy, lukewarm, wanting to sit on the fence, be a spectator, and concerned about other people's opinion. I valued his forgiveness, his grace, and his mercy way too much. I valued the love I felt, and I wanted this newfound friendship with him to continue to grow. I was still looking for the joy like "none other has ever known."

Through many small group Bible studies over the next couple of years, I learned that when we give our heart to Christ, something happens: "Therefore, if anyone is in Christ, the new creation has come: The old has gone, the new is here" (2 Corinthians 5:17, niv). What is this new creation? What does it look like? Would this new creation help me to deal with my pride? From what I gathered, the "new creation" is not some sort of outward transformation. Rather, there is a change in character and conduct. And more than that, when a believer surrenders his or her whole life to the will of God through Jesus Christ, a new heart is given to this new creation. We become God's workmanship. He places a desire within us, a hunger and a thirst, to know him and to love him above all things. In the Holy Book, the Lord makes the promise, "And I will give you a new heart, and I will put a new spirit in you. I will take out your stony, stubborn heart and give you a tender, responsive heart" (Ezekiel 36:26, nlt).

Furthermore, God tells us he knows something about us that

we do not like to hear, to acknowledge, or even to admit about ourselves. He tells us, "The heart is deceitful above all things..." (Jeremiah 17:9, niv). What now? I had just given my heart to God and he is telling me that it is deceitful! If a friend or a family member told me my heart is deceitful, I would definitely be offended. But when Almighty God tells me my heart is "deceitful above all things," it is like another awareness in his mirror of truth. This is the awareness I must face day to day in order to walk in union with him. This is the challenge, the hard part for us humans—that is, to face the hardcore truths about our inner selves, to forget what others might think about us, and to concern ourselves with seeking God's approval above any other.

*　*　*

I will never forget, nor can I diminish the desire, the hunger, and thirst to know the Lord that began to sweep over me. My husband used to tease that he goes to bed with not only me, but also Abraham, Isaac, Jacob, Moses, and many other people within the Holy Book because I am always reading, devouring, and absorbing all that I can wrap my mind around. It was like awakening from a long winter's sleep wondering what have I missed out on all this time, and how can I possibly catch up? It was also like finding a cave full of treasure. Each fragment I picked up was more beautiful and more precious than the last, each one causing me to touch, to explore, to feel with every one of my five senses. If you have ever explored a magnificent cave in a mountain region, you will know what I mean.

It also reminded me of a game we played when we were kids. Pretending we were going on a great adventure to a far-off land, we would take our little red wagon—the one Father had built a wooden box on for the purpose of hauling wood. Loading it with our two younger siblings, we would take off down the lane arguing over who was going to be "leader in charge" of this adventure. But it didn't matter; we were so excited about the adventure. Soon we would come across an imaginary mountain peak with an odd-looking stone door seeming to invite us in. Yet we did not know the passcode, so we would yell out in a deep, throaty voice, "Open Sesame!" just like we had read in the fable

Ali Baba and the Forty Thieves. As if by magic the stone door opened, and we walked inside with our mouths wide open, oohing and awing. Pretending to see many imaginary treasures, we would run about capturing armfuls of imaginary gold and silver (these were actually apples that had fallen from the trees in the orchard), all that we could carry, until we reached our fullness. *Just like children,* I thought. And that is how God wants us to come to him, with the open hands, arms, hearts, and minds of innocent little children, believing we can capture "immeasurably more than all we ask or imagine" (Ephesians 3:20, niv). Even the apostle Paul believed this as he prayed for his fellow Ephesians:

> *For this reason I kneel before the Father, from whom his whole family in heaven and on earth derives its name. I pray that out of his glorious riches he may strengthen you with power through his Spirit in your inner being, so that Christ may dwell in your hearts through faith. And I pray that you, being rooted and established in love, may have power, together with all the saints, to grasp how wide and long and high and deep is the*

love of Christ, and to know this love that surpasses knowledge-

that you may be filled to the measure of all the fullness of God.

—Ephesians 3:14–19, niv

Now I was beginning to believe that the study of the Holy Book, God's Word to us, his written love letter, was one of the highest, mysterious, exciting, and most intellectual pursuits anyone could possibly undertake. It made me wonder how anyone could reasonably spend their time studying anything else, reading anything else, watching anything else when we have this amazing story about God, about his great love for us, and about the terrific lengths he goes to be in relationship with us.

One night as I was plumbing the depths of the Holy Book, I read how Jesus had promised his disciples, upon his departure, that he would send the Comforter, the Holy Spirit to help them: "But the Advocate, the Holy Spirit, whom the Father will send in my name, will teach you all things and will remind you of everything I have said to you" (John 14:26, niv). And also, "When the Advocate comes, whom I will send to you from the Father— the Spirit of truth who goes out from the Father—he will testify about me" (John 15:16, niv). I continued to read on into the book of Acts, the first chapter. Following his resurrection, Jesus was meeting with his disciples. "On one occasion, while he was eating with them, he gave them this command: 'do not leave Jerusalem, but wait for the gift my Father promised, which you have heard me speak about. For John baptized with water, but in a few days you will be baptized with the Holy Spirit'" (Acts 1:4–5, niv).

I remember praying and asking the Lord, how does one receive the Holy Spirit? And had I already received the Holy Spirit when this hunger and thirst for knowledge came over me? If not, can I receive the Holy Spirit also? As I prayed, I earnestly asked God to send the Holy Spirit to be my Advocate, my Teacher, the Spirit of Truth in my life, to be my Comforter, and my Helper. You see, I knew I could not love God "with all my heart, mind, and strength" without supernatural help from his Spirit, because I knew my heart was, as he had said, truly deceitful, and I recognized my own level of self-centeredness—it was pretty high. "I do need this kind of help," I assured God.

As I prayed, I opened my Bible to see if God might have a

message for me. It opened to Second Kings. Now I had never read anything in Second Kings and didn't even know what it was about. But there on the pages was a conversation between Elijah and Elisha. Elijah, who was a notable prophet in Israel, was also a loving mentor and teacher to Elisha. Elijah was going away to be with the Lord but asked Elisha, "Tell me what can I do for you before I am taken from you?" "Let me inherit a double portion of your spirit," Elisha replied. "You have asked a difficult thing," Elijah said, "yet if you see me when I am taken from you, it will be yours…" (2 Kings 9–10, niv).

While I peered into their conversation as if I were eavesdropping, I immediately thought, *Oh, my gosh! I am going to receive a double portion of God's Holy Spirit.* I got so excited my heart did a flip-flop just like it did on the day I had received the "voice" and the "vision" about the Miss World and about sharing the stage with Bob Hope. God had absolutely made that vision come true. Would he also make this message come true? I waited in great expectation over the next few days and weeks to see how this might manifest itself. I was expecting some great and mighty changes to take place in my life. I was expecting to receive a supernatural love and a joy like "none other has ever known." Instead, all that was happening to me was an overwhelming sense of sadness and sudden tearful episodes that came in waves. It felt like I was going through a grieving process, as if I had lost a dear friend or loved one. I couldn't understand it and thought I was actually slipping into a state of depression. Then one morning, I was leaving the house. As I got into my car, I heard a female speaker on a Christian radio station say, "If you are crying about something, let it flow, no matter how long it takes. Crying is God's way of purifying our hearts."

Really? I thought. *Is that what is happening to me? Is God purifying my heart?* And so I did. I let the tears flow. For days the tears flowed. I cried about the hardships and the loss of my childhood, not only for me but also for my sisters and brothers. I cried about my lost innocence at the hands of a pedophile. I cried for the other young girls who might have suffered and are still suffering as I did. I cried about the loss of my home and my personal identity. I cried because I failed to be the goodwill ambassador to Prince Edward Island that many had expected of me. I cried about the loss of my first love. I cried about the loss of my first marriage and the pain caused to our daughter by both me and her father. I cried about the pain caused to my stepchildren by my second marriage. I cried about my own lack of wisdom and my responsibility in the choices I had made that caused harm and pain to others. I cried about the sins I had committed, sins that I knew were committed in disobedience to my Heavenly Father. And finally I cried because I had been unable to forgive myself all these years. I felt condemned. I had not yet allowed the truth of the resurrection to wash over me and give me freedom. Jesus said, "If you hold to my teaching…then you will know the truth, and the truth will set you free" (John 8:31–32, niv). "Let your truth wash me and set me free," I prayed.

As I wept for several days, I could feel the washing and the purifying taking place in my heart. When I was done, there was no longer any sadness nor any sign of depression. The crying was finished. Amazingly, I have never cried like that since. I realized what had just happened: I had invited Jesus to come live in my heart. But he was showing me, through a very powerful and physical manifestation, "You invited me into your heart, but you are not letting me in. There is no room for me. It is all tied up. It is full." In order to make space for him, I needed to receive a double portion of his spirit, a double cleansing; or as Mother would say when we came in from working in the potato fields, "You need a double scrubbing!"

After I received this "double scrubbing," there was now room for Jesus. He was able to pour out more of himself as he promises to do, taking up permanent residence in my heart, sitting on the throne of my heart. Through the power of the Holy Spirit, I began to recognize the valuable gifts God offers us when we give our all to Jesus—a "purpose and a plan" for our lives, "the right to be called children of God," and the promise of "eternal life." I noticed a sense of freedom from my own condemnation. Now I was fully understanding the purpose of Jesus's death and resurrection. I was free! What a beautiful and glorious heart victory, just as precious as the heart victories I received with Mother and Father many years ago; but this time, the heart victory was both precious and powerful. Thanks to the work of the Holy Spirit, my Helper, I started to grasp the height, the depth, the breadth, and the width of Christ's love for me—a love that surpasses knowledge, as Paul said when he prayed for his Ephesian family.

* * *

Not wanting to lose the benefits received from my "double scrubbing," I began to bathe myself in his love—morning, noon, and night—learning many more fascinating things. I was eager to experience the depths of his love while understanding new words that were currently foremost in my mind, words such as "trust," "freedom," "submission," "obedience," "humility," "fulfillment of the law," "abiding in Christ," and so on. From Paul's letter to the Galatians I read, "You, my brothers and sisters, were called to be free. But do not use your freedom to indulge the flesh; rather, serve one another humbly in love. For the entire law is fulfilled in keeping this one command: 'Love your neighbor as yourself. If you bite and devour each other, watch out or you will be destroyed by each other'" (Galatians 5: 13–15, niv). This lesson was a reminder of what Mother would tell us as children when we were constantly quarreling, "You children must learn to get along. You need to love one another and be kind to one another." My mother was not a churchgoing woman nor was she educated in biblical principles, but it is interesting to note that she knew and understood divine principles that were passed on to her from her parents, absolute truths from God that we as children/individuals/neighbors must learn to love one another. I feel these divine principles and absolute, universal truths are being lost to a great extent in today's secular culture. How I wish all humanity could learn to love one another as Christ loves us with his sacrificial love.

This love that "surpasses knowledge" was taking hold in my heart and my soul. I believe, as Paul wrote, that Christ's love "surpasses knowledge" because it is more beautiful than anything I have ever experienced and so magnificent I have difficulty putting it into words. I was indeed changing, becoming a new creature, as the Lord promises. That is how we know, beyond a doubt, because of the overwhelming changes taking place in our hearts, in our lives, and in our circumstances.

The pain of my past difficulties was now a distant memory just like when I gave birth and became a mother. I immediately forgot the pain of labor once I held my precious newborn baby in my arms. I became overwhelmed with this pure, undefiled, outrageous, and unconditional love for my child. Knowing and understanding God's love for us in this way is truly life-changing. And his love is not limited in any way—amazingly. "God has poured out his love into our hearts by the Holy Spirit, whom he has given us" (Romans 5:5, niv). Also, amazingly, he "pours out" more than just his love, for as Paul says, "The grace of our Lord was poured out on me abundantly, along with the faith and love that are in Christ Jesus" (1 Timothy 1:14, niv).

As I became more and more acquainted with this "love that surpasses knowledge," along with the "abundant pouring out" of grace and faith from the Holy Spirit, I started to feel a sense of deep gratitude for everything, no matter what my circumstances. Suffice it to say, no one—and I mean no one—has perfect circumstances. We all face trials and tribulations, successes and failures in our lives, often on a daily basis. However, as we yield to the Spirit, we understand it is God's way of developing our character, our persistence, and our hope. With a grateful heart, we can see even the smallest blessings, even the smallest ordinary miracles occurring, sometimes lasting for just a moment or two; but when they happen, we thank God for them. Before long, we will be looking at our lives, our relationships, our circumstances with new eyes, and we will "not be anxious about anything" (Philippians 4:6, niv). Additionally, our thoughts will change. We will "rejoice in the Lord always. I will say it again: Rejoice! Let your gentleness be evident to all ... whatever is true, whatever is noble, whatever is right, whatever is pure, whatever is lovely, whatever is admirable—if anything is excellent or praiseworthy—think about such things" (Philippians 4:4, 8, niv). This is how God works in us; he fills us to fullness when we learn his ways.

With a grateful heart and with spiritual eyes on God, the fruit of the Spirit multiplies a hundredfold. And what is the fruit of the Spirit? "But the fruit of the Spirit is love, joy, peace, patience, kindness, goodness, faithfulness, gentleness and self-control" (Galatians 5:22, niv). I thought, *Who doesn't want these wonderful characteristics, these qualities in their life? I certainly do! And who doesn't want them to multiply and grow into the kind of characteristics that Jesus himself displayed, a kind of purity, a kind of holiness in our preparation for eternal life with him? I certainly do!*

Over the next few months I continued to walk in step with Jesus, abiding in him like a vine abides in a tree that is deeply rooted. Before long, I began to experience an amazing joy like "none other has ever known." It was a quiet joy, but it was steady, unwavering, and consistent. I tested it over time. I wanted to make sure it was not going to leave me like happiness does. Happiness is dependent upon momentary circumstances, but joy can be lasting, even in the midst of extremely difficult times. When my husband had a serious car accident that left him completely dependent for several months, my joy did not dissipate. I knew without a doubt that the divine presence of God was with me—this time more powerfully than when I was a young teenager. This time it was with a deeper understanding of God's qualities, God's characteristics, and God's will for his children. This time I knew and understood the role of the Trinity: God the Father, Jesus the Son, and the Holy Spirit as our Helper—all of the Trinity working together, in union, to bring the learning process and our salvation experience to its fulfillment. I realized this was the knowledge that had been missing when I went through "the dark night of the soul." If we all find this deeper understanding of God, we can all avoid the terrible pitfalls that I went through.

In addition, I could feel my level of patience, my kindness, and goodness growing within my spirit and within my conduct. I knew without a doubt that this kind of change was not from me. It had to be coming from the outpouring of the Spirit within me, changing me, because in my humanness I was way too selfish, stubborn, impatient, and unkind. However, Jesus says, "I am the vine; you are the branches. If a man remains in me and I in him, he will bear much fruit; apart from me you can do nothing"

(John 15:5, niv). I knew this to be true, that apart from Jesus I was totally incapable of acting and being this way. Apart from Jesus I could "do nothing." I was incapable of sacrificial love like he expresses, "Greater love has no one than this, that he lay down his life for his friends. You are my friends...I have called you friends, for everything that I learned from my Father I have made known to you" (John 15:13–15, niv).

What joy! Jesus just called me "his friend!" I realized I was actually in this unbelievable personal relationship with Jesus just like Father had experienced. "And he walks with me, and he talks with me, and he tells me I am his own. And the joy we share, as we tarry there, none other has ever known." Making the connection to this Source reminded me of seeing, on television, a spacecraft going through space and docking with the mother space station. As you watch the approach, you can almost hear the "click" once the connection is made. It locks on. You know beyond a doubt that you have reached your destination. Once there it continues to refuel, like an unending fountain, filling you up every day and bubbling forth, overflowing from your belly. My link with a "love that surpasses knowledge" and my human fulfillment, my fullness is more than complete. The young girl who persisted in rubbing the frosty window with her little fingers, waiting, searching, and yearning has now found her fulfillment in Christ. The island girl who travelled around the world looking into the faces of the rich and famous, the elderly and sick, searching for meaning and purpose, has now reached the true shoreline. The undertow is completely gone.

Thank you, Jesus, for showing me that every life is valuable and significant to you. Thank you, Father, for your legacy that led me to search for spiritual significance and personal value in the living Lord. Thank you for leading me in your footsteps through the storms of life so I could find this divine treasure capable of transforming my heart, and giving me this triumphant inheritance for my spirit. Thank you, Mother, for teaching me persistence, determination, internal beauty, and the will to love others. Through both of you—your teachings, guidance, and leading—I have come home! What glorious contentment!

Yes, I have now found the place my heart calls home. The

search is over. I no longer need to "tap my heels together three times" in order to be transferred or to find escape from one situation to another. I now know who I am—a child of the living Lord who has the right to enter his throne room at any time, to just sit and love my Heavenly Father, to thank him and praise him all day long. I now know where I belong—exactly where God has placed me within the circumstances of my life, to live and learn and grow in sacrificial love, in grace, and in faith as it is poured out abundantly onto me day by day. I now know what my purpose is in life—to be an "ambassador for Christ" and to share my knowledge of his great love with others, not to force it on others but to share with those who have a desire to hear and to grow and to find the divine treasures, their true destiny, just as I did. Sharing his love with others is one of the greatest gifts God has given to me—one that also gives me extreme joy.

Our destiny is our eternal home in heaven, "the kingdom of ideal beauty" provided to us through the cross of Christ. In this life, our name may or may not appear on a marquis or be written in lights; but in heaven, our name is written in the royal book of life forever. In this life, we might achieve a few minutes of fame; but those lights will only grow dim, whereas the lights of our heavenly home will constantly grow brighter. In this life we may amass a few treasures, but in heaven, we will have a great inheritance for we "received a Spirit of sonship. And by him we cry, "Abba, Father." The Spirit himself testifies with our spirit that we are God's children. Now if we are children, then we are heirs—heirs of God and co-heirs with Christ, if indeed we share in his sufferings in order that we may also share in his glory" (Romans 8: 15b–17, niv). In this life we may lose our position serving a number of years in one career, or a title may be taken from us after one year, but in heaven, our position with Christ is guaranteed. "Having believed, you were marked in him with a seal, the promised Holy Spirit, who is a deposit guaranteeing our inheritance ... to the praise of his glory" (Ephesians 1: 13–14, niv).

To the praise of his glory, in this life God will take all our current pain, sufferings, mistakes, circumstances, and the consequences we endure from past mistakes; and he will "work all things together for the good of those who love him, who have been called according to his purpose" (Romans 8: 28, niv). To the praise of his glory, when we reach our destiny there will be no more suffering, for in heaven, "He will wipe every tear from their eyes. There will be no more death or mourning or crying or pain" (Revelation 21:4, niv). To the praise of his glory, it is he who "bestows a crown of beauty…for the display of his spendor" (Isaiah 61:3, niv) and not for our own.

What victory! What glorious triumph! Like King Solomon, a man who had everything including wisdom, power, and wealth— a man who tried everything to find meaning and purpose in life just like I did—he studied, he led, he tried pleasure, he tried work, he denied himself nothing that he desired. He tried "everything under the sun" and found it all to be meaningless, "a chasing after the wind." He came to this conclusion: "Meaningless! Meaningless!" says the Teacher. "Everything is meaningless!" (Ecclesiastes 12:8, niv) And so it is for me; all my pursuits to find meaning and purpose were meaningless compared to finding, keeping, and nurturing a true friendship with the Lord. Along with King Solomon, I can fully declare,

Of making many books there is no end, and much study wearies the body. Now all has been heard; here is the conclusion of the matter: Fear God and keep his commandments, for this is the whole duty of man. For God will bring every deed into judgment, including every hidden thing, whether it is good or evil.
—ECCLESIASTES 12:13–14, NIV

Finally my heart is at home, my joy is complete, and my spirit soars in triumph as I sit contentedly on the true shoreline, nestled within the shelter of my Heavenly Father. The triumphant spirit realizes there is nothing in this world more valuable than the love of Christ and that nothing, nothing can ever separate us from his love. This is my wish for you, the reader, to find this glorious heart victory for yourself and to find this triumphant love for your spirit—a love that surpasses knowledge, a love that is everlasting, a love that never fails, for he is "the Alpha and

the Omega, the First and the Last, the Beginning and the End"
(Revelation 22:13, niv). There is no substitute. No, not one.

No, in all these things we are more than conquerors through him who loved us. For I am convinced that neither death nor life, neither angels nor demons, neither the present nor the future, nor any powers, neither height nor depth, nor anything else in all creation, will be able to separate us from the love of God that is in Christ Jesus our Lord.

—ROMANS 9:37–39 (NIV)

THE NEXT GENERATION

My mouth will tell of your righteous deeds,
of your saving acts all day long—
though I know not how to relate them all.
I will come and proclaim your mighty acts, Sovereign Lord;
I will proclaim your righteous deeds, yours alone.
Since my youth, God, you have taught me,
and to this day I declare your marvelous deeds.
Even when I am old and gray,
do not forsake me, my God,
till I declare your power to the next generation,
your mighty acts to all who are to come.

—PSALM 71:15–18 (NIV)

My book *Island Girl: A Triumph of the Spirit* was first released in August 2015—three years ago already! How time flies! Yet I continue to tell of God's righteous deeds and his saving acts even when I don't know how to relate them all. There are so many.

Shortly after the release of my book in 2015, the publisher Tate Publishing, Inc. went out of business and my book out of circulation. Yet, God saved my story by leading me to a great publisher in Nashville, Tennessee—Elm Hill, an imprint of Thomas Nelson. Elm Hill and Thomas Nelson are registered trademarks of HarperCollins Christian Publishing, Inc. To have such a dynamic publisher stand with me and my work is not only comforting, it is encouraging. I am encouraged because my heart burns within me to share God's story, to declare his power and his glory to the next generation.

One critique I received from the original release of the book was, "I wish you had told more stories about the pageants and not so much of the spiritual journey." My response is that *Island Girl: A Triumph of the Spirit* is not about me. The book is about

God. It is his story. It is about his amazing power at work in the life of a young girl. It is about the depths he went to so that I could find my identity in him and not in the glitz and glamour of the world. It is about solving and resolving my identity crisis in a personal relationship with Christ.

Friends, if you missed this point with the first read then I encourage you to read the book again. *Psychology Today* states that seventy percent of women and girls are in a personal identity crisis. Suicide rates among teens are growing. Runaways, sexual abuse, and sex trafficking of girls and boys are on the rise. Drug addiction and heroin use is at an all-time high. Many babies require detoxification upon birth. Our lives, our culture are all mixed up. In many cases, we tear each other down instead of building each other up.

These circumstances are not God's will for you. God wants you to discover him through your trials and journeys as I did. He wants you to experience the height, depth, breadth, and width of his love for you. He invites you to join his family. Read and reread this story again and again until you too find the restoration that I found. Look for these heart victories in your life.

Another saving act of God in reference to my book is that he has opened the door and paved the way for me to enter into a contract with a screenwriter. This screenwriter sees my story as a potential faith-based, inspirational movie. Will this ever happen? That is a question that is yet to be answered. This is a major step in my journey and it requires much learning. Many things have to fall into place: finding a producer willing to take on the project, finding an executive producer willing to raise the necessary funds, finding an entertainment attorney and an intellectual property attorney to protect the work and the story. Again, will this ever happen? I don't know! But one thing I have learned in my walk with the Lord is that "if it is in his will, then it will happen." Only he knows. I remain amazed at how he has already used a poor farm girl from Prince Edward Island. I just follow along as if I am on a great adventure with him. Please pray for his continued leading. I see this opportunity as another effective way to "declare his power to the next generation."

* * *

In addition to the above "righteous deeds and saving acts of God" over the last three years, he has also continued to work in my heart. His cleansing process does not end until we meet him face to face. We must remain open to his work and see what mighty lessons he continues to teach us.

Daily living had become difficult for me and my husband over the past several years. His recent death compounded my emotional wellbeing. Bill had developed several health issues. It all started December 08, 2010. The phone rang. It was a police officer saying, "Your husband has been in a car accident. It does not appear to be too serious. He just has a bump on the head." I instructed the officer to send him to a hospital close to our home. I would meet him there.

I waited and waited in the ER, but the ambulance did not arrive. Finally I learned that things were much more serious than they realized. He had been transported to the trauma center at another location.

Fear, panic, worry set in. Heart cries—times when we have

so much chaos in our life's circumstances that we cry out to God to help us. We've all experienced them. Learning to walk on the chaos of heart cries with God is such a faith-building experience. It causes us to surrender our will to his providence when we recognize our need for him; when we fall into the beauty of his loving arms, into the protection of his power to see us through our heart cries. Heart cries are the trials God allows in our lives to lead us toward spiritual heart victories.

In my book *Island Girl: A Triumph of the Spirit*, I share several of my heart victories. Heart victories are the triumphant life lessons we learn during our difficult heart cries; the lightbulb comes on and we have those ah-ha moments to see more clearly. These victories shine a brighter light into our character. They are teaching tools used by God to develop more persistence and giving us greater hope and wisdom. In other words, they make us stronger in our faith and in our life. Our goal in any of our trials is to discover these heart victories. I believe we discover them best in relationship with God as our teacher.

We all journey through heart cries in various ways. God

knows which lesson each of us must learn. He knows how to shape our character whereby we reach that magical moment of surrender, a level of brokenness when we rely on him, recognize our need for him and give our life over to him.

Did you know this is our perfect sacrifice? It is the sacrifice God loves more than anything else we can offer him. In the Psalms, King David wrote, "My sacrifice, O God, is a broken spirit; a broken and contrite heart you God, will not despise" (Psalm 51:17, niv). This was the great King David's heart cry to God after he had become completely broken through his own sin and poor life choices. King David knew that the God he cried out to would not despise his brokenness, but rather embrace his sincere repentance. Because of his broken heart and broken spirit sacrifice, David became special in God's eyes. Just think about that—one who committed adultery and murder would be called "a man after God's own heart."

While writing *Island Girl: A Triumph of the Spirit*, I thought I had already reached the end of myself and had given all my brokenness to God. I thought I had learned all that God was going to reveal to me about his character. However, when God placed me in the position of caring for my husband over the last seven years and I cried out to him with this new heart cry, I learned depths of God's love, joy, peace, patience, kindness, goodness, gentleness, faithfulness and self-control—depths I never knew I was capable of achieving. These lessons did not happen suddenly or all at once. They were learned with great difficulty, with a desire to run and hide, with a desire to reject the lessons and avoid them altogether. There were times when I begged God "to take this cup from me" as Christ did in the Garden of Gethsemane. But God never let me go. He walked on the chaos with me just as Jesus had walked on the waves during the storm with his disciples.

One day, six years after that dreadful car accident, my husband and I were sitting together. He had reached his place of brokenness—a place where he could no longer walk; where he needed assistance with all activities of daily living; where he had lost his strength and virility; where he had lost his words and was approaching bedridden status. He looked at me and said, "I just feel like crying."

My response surprised both of us. "Can I cry for you?" I asked with deep concern. He nodded his head, his lips quivering.

Looking into his eyes I saw this raw, fervent, unrestrained pain, and the compassion that had been Jesus' compassion washed over me. I wept for my husband just as I am sure Jesus wept for his friend Lazarus. I felt a level of compassion that was so deep I came to understand the shortest verse in the Bible, "Jesus wept" (John 11:35 NIV). Immediately I realized that allowing God to do his work in us, sensing his experiences, sensing his own pain, is an incredible experience.

It was in these tender moments with my husband that I knew why God had placed me in these circumstances. He wanted to teach me about this level of compassion.

Have you ever had a spiritual heart victory like this? Have you ever been so affected by something that you rejoice in your brokenness and difficulty? Have you ever been so affected that you give thanks to God for the suffering and want to shout out to the whole world, "Praise God for his love, mercy, grace and kindness amidst your pain?"

He wants me to offer my insights to those who are in similar trying circumstances, to those whose heart cries out to him daily for strength and patience. I believe God is leading me and trusting me to share this compassionate love experience with you. I believe that is why he has placed such a burning fire in my heart to "declare his power to the next generation." Our world is missing out on this compassionate love. Jesus wants us to look at one another and say, "Can I cry for you?"

Can we cry for one another, for the next generation?

APPENDIX A

FATHER'S WAR RECORD

Father, age 21; not in full military dress

Corporal Charles Hartwell Hickey (F77762), was born in Darnley, Prince Edward Island, on September 2, 1919, son of James W. Hickey and wife Annie Abbot. He attended Darnley school and helped on the family farm during summer holidays. On completing his formal education, he worked with the Woodside family on the Ray Woodside Fox Ranch.

Hickey served two years as a reservist prior to WWII, having enlisted in Charlottetown on September 3, 1939. Assigned to the PEI Highlanders, he took his basic training at Beach Grove Inn, PEI. He was admitted to full service on April 3, 1941, and transferred to the PEI Light Horse for additional training.

Corporal Hickey spent his embarkation leave at his home in Darnley prior to posting to Camp Borden, PEI, where he was trained in trucks, tanks, Bren Gun Carriers, and motorcycles. On November 11, 1941, he was TOS (taken on strength) and shipped overseas via Halifax, Canada, to Liverpool, England, on a troop ship that zigzagged across the Atlantic, changing course every so many minutes to avoid being torpedoed. However, the ship, which was escorted by destroyers, struck a mine en route.

It took on water, but the crew succeeded in repairing the damage sufficiently to sail up the River Mersey after seventeen days at sea. "It was probably the bitterest cold we had ever experienced as we sailed into the North Atlantic, experiencing ferocious seas along the way."

Hickey was stationed at both Aldershot and Henley Downs, where he developed sinus trouble. Shortly thereafter he was handed his discharge papers to return to Canada along with other soldiers. Wishing to escape being sent home, he hid in an air raid shelter for three days. Within three days, the corvette carrying the other men home was torpedoed.

Later Hickey was posted to Farnborough for tank training on a seven-month course. Transferred to Brighton, he was billeted in the city for three days prior to boarding a ship with the intention of participating in the Dieppe Raid. The ship, which carried men, tanks, and equipment, was recalled at approximately eight miles, consequently aborting their part in the raid.

Corporal Hickey landed on the Coast of France on the eighth day after D-Day on June 6, 1944, with No. 2 Corps Headquarters.

A beachhead had already been established; nevertheless, losses were heavy from aerial bombing. Here Hickey witnessed the horror of seeing the shore lined with the bodies of dead servicemen. Getting trucks off the landing craft was a dangerous and delicate operation, as in some instances men were up to their necks in the water. Once ashore, however, they headed inland, rapidly covering two-and-one-half miles. At one point, they were pinned down for several days by enemy fire. Eventually breaking out, they started to advance and take prisoners.

Hickey recalls, "The Battle of Caen was ferocious. We were held down for sometime. We lost a lot of men, our ammunition, and petrol dump. After that, the advance was steady via Denmark. Engineers replaced the bridges as we progressed forward."

Corporal Hickey's responsibilities included driving for the orderly room and operating a water truck, which carried a motorcycle. At one point while on his way to the rear corps, his motorcycle rolled, and he fractured his left tibia. At another time, he was ordered to take forty replacements to the front where the casualties were heavy. On another occasion, he captured two German soldiers about seventeen to eighteen years of age. Taking them prisoners, he turned them over to the medical officer.

About eight miles from Berlin, word came that the war was over. However, not everyone had received the word, and there was still some sporadic fighting going on for a time.

Several weeks after V-Day on May 8, 1945, Hickey was transferred back to Farnborough in England and returned home a few weeks later via Halifax on the Queen Elizabeth. He received his discharge on December 17, 1945, subsequently spending two years in the reserve army as corporal instructor on tanks and Bren Gun Carriers. Hickey received the Canadian Volunteer Service Medal, the 1939-1945 Star, the War Medal 1939-1945, the Defence Medal and the France and Germany Star.

On a personal note, upon returning permanently to civilian life in 1947, Hickey purchased his farm in Darnley through the auspices of the Veteran's Land Act. He farmed for a number of years, then drove a school bus for seventeen years.

Charles married Marion Barbara Stewart of Hamilton, PEI, on August 15, 1947. Mrs. Hickey is herself a veteran with three-and-one-half years with the Royal Canadian Air Force Women's Division. The Hickeys lived in Darnley prior to Mr. Hickey's death in 1986. They had ten children—seven girls and three boys.

To learn more about the Canadian War Efforts, the D-Day Northwest European Invasion of Normandy and the Battle of Caen, please refer to "Military history of Canada during World War II," Wikipedia contributors, Wikipedia, The Free Encyclopedia, last modified August 3, 2014, http://en.wikipedia. org/w/index. php?title=Military_history_of_Canada_during_ World_War_II&oldid=619676471.

Father, age 67. He died December 23, 1986 from lung cancer.

APPENDIX B

MOTHER'S WAR RECORD

Mother, age 20, in full military dress

AW2 Marion Barbara Stewart (W314287) was born in
Hamilton, Prince Edward Island, on April 26, 1923,
daughter of Elizabeth (Owen) and Byron Stewart. She attended
Hamilton School.

Upon graduation, she took a seven-month clerical course
and worked in Ottawa, Ontario, at A. Workman & Co. as a cashier and typist.

Stewart served the Royal Canadian Air Force from October
29, 1943 to December 3, 1946, in the Ottawa, Ontario, office. She
worked on clerical administrative duties pertaining to the organization and administration of the Air Force. She also worked on
a teleprinter, sending and receiving messages. Upon receiving
her discharge in December 1946, she returned to Hamilton, PEI.
Stewart received both the Canadian Volunteer Service Medal
and the War Medal 1939–45.

On a personal note, she married Charles Hartwell Hickey on
August 15, 1947. They had ten children—seven girls and three
boys. Upon her death, August 16, 2013, at the age of ninety,

this matriarch had twenty-four grandchildren and thirty-five great-grandchildren.

Mother on her ninetieth birthday, April 26, 2013. (Photo by Barb Hickey Photography, Kensington, PEI, Canada.).

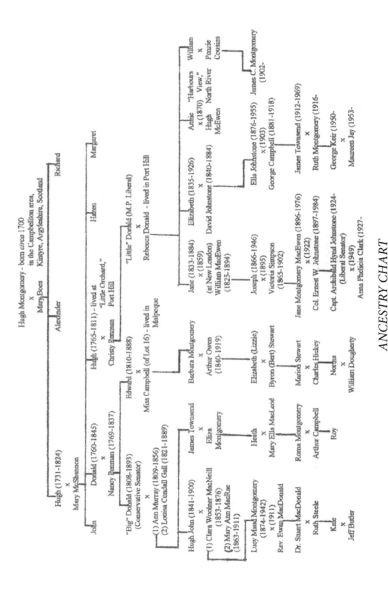

ANCESTRY CHART

Author's Final Notes

To learn more about Norma Joyce and her large family, visit her webpage: normajdougherty.com and follow her on Facebook, Twitter, LinkedIn, Google Plus, and Pinterest.

To discover many more interesting facts about Prince Edward Island, visit the webpage: PEI Tourism. See why PEI is rated by Condé Nast Traveler as one of the top islands to visit.

To visit the "little white church with the majestic steeple," go to the webpage: Princetown United Church, Malpeque, Prince Edward Island.

Photo by: Norma Pasatieri, Malpeque, Prince Edward Island, Canada

Stonecroft Ministries, Inc.

To learn more about the women's ministry that influenced Norma's life and helped her understand the scriptures through easy, applicable Stonecroft Bible Studies, visit the website: stonecroft.org.

Norma comments, "I love the way this ministry invites you into the Word of God." As their website states:

"Whatever you've done, wherever you've been, God wants to be discovered by you! He has made Himself known in His Word—the Bible. Whether the Bible is familiar or new to you, its contents will transform your life and bring answers to life's questions.

Gather with people in your communities—women, men, couples, young and old alike—and explore together what the Bible says about Jesus Christ. Stonecroft Bible Studies reveal His life, His values, His wonder, and His words. Each study includes discussion questions for riveting conversation, specific Scripture to investigate, and time for prayer.

Stonecroft Bible Studies include page numbers with scripture references in keeping with Stonecroft's commitment to produce biblical material for those not familiar with the Bible. The scripture references in these studies point to verses in the Abundant Life Bible, New Living Translation. Gather together your friends, neighbors, family members, and others to discover more of God through these small-group explorations of the Bible." (Used by permission of Lorraine Potter Kalal, President and CEO, Stonecroft Ministries.)

Norma adds, "How easy is that? Stonecroft is making these studies so easy, they have even matched the study book reference pages to the Bible that is used. There is no fault-finding in these groups and there is no criticism for "not knowing" what you do not yet know. Reminds me of another scripture verse from the Holy Book!"

"If any of you lacks wisdom, you should ask God, who gives generously to all without finding fault, and it will be given to you" James 1:5 (niv).

As Stonecroft Ministries says, "God wants to be discovered by you!" Do seek Him as I did. Your life will never be the same, I promise!

In Christ's precious love,

Norma

CPSIA information can be obtained
at www.ICGtesting.com
Printed in the USA
LVHW032118071218
599704LV00010B/30